Contemporary's
Essentials of
Reading

Book 4

McGraw Hill **Wright Group**

Photo and Art Credits

Computer art created by Jim Blanton; Cover Mark Burnett; 5 Mark Burnett;
12 Bob Daemmrich Photo, Inc.; 22, 29 Mark Burnett; 30 Elaine Shay; 37 Tim Courlas;
42 Gerard Photography; 51 Mark Burnett; 61 Doug Martin; 62, 70, 80 Aaron Haupt;
88 KS Studios; 96 Mark Burnett; 107 Steve Allen/Gamma-Liaison;
108, 109 Archive Photos.

Permission Acknowledgment

"Alone" From OH PRAY MY WINGS ARE GONNA FIT ME WELL by Maya Angelou
Copyright © 1975 by Maya Angelou.
Reprinted by permission of Random House, Inc.

"Woman Work" From AND STILL I RISE by Maya Angelou
Copyright © 1978 by Maya Angelou.
Reprinted by permission of Random House, Inc.

"I, Too" From COLLECTED POEMS by Langston Hughes
Copyright © 1994 by the Estate of Langston Hughes.
Reprinted by permission of Alfred A Knopf Inc

From THE POETRY OF ROBERT FROST,
edited by Edward Connery Lathem. 1951 by Robert Frost,
© copyright 1923, © 1969 by Henry Holt & Co., Inc.
Reprinted by permission of Henry Holt & Co., Inc.

From Daniels, Jim. PLACES/EVERYONE. Copyright 1985.
Winner of the 1985 Brittingham Prize in Poetry.
Reprinted by permissions of the University of Wisconsin Press.

"Want Ads—Employment Opportunities" by Robert Garrison,
from GOING FOR COFFEE
Copyright © 1981 by Tom Wayman

Wright Group

ISBN: 0-07-282263-5

Send all inquiries to:
Wright Group/McGraw-Hill
130 E. Randolph, Suite 400
Chicago, IL 60601

Printed in the United States of America.

2 3 4 5 6 7 8 9 10 QPD 08 07 06 05 04

The editorial staff wishes to gratefully acknowledge the contributions of the following advisors, reviewers, and writers, whose considerable efforts, suggestions, ideas, and insights helped to make this series a more valuable and viable learning tool.

Advisory Board for the *McGraw-Hill/Contemporary Essentials of Reading Series*

JoAnn Bukovich-Henderson
Director,
SE Regional Resource Center
Juneau, Alaska

Dr. William Walker
Assistant Superintendant,
Adult Basic Education
Knox County Schools
Knoxville, Tennessee

Nancy Wilson-Webb
Co-op Director of
   Adult Basic Education
Fort Worth ISD Consortium
Fort Worth, Texas

Contributing Writers

Jeanne M. Lance
Program Coordinator
Ohio Family Literacy
Statewide Initiative
Ohio Department of Education
Columbus, Ohio

Clarita D. Henderson
Educational Consultant
Buffalo City Schools
Buffalo, New York

Dr. Nancy Burkhalter
Language and Literacy Consultant
Laramie, Wyoming

Mary Frances Harper
ABE Educator
Sheridan, Arkansas

Carole Gerber
Columbus, Ohio

Doug Hutzelman
Kettering, Ohio

Regan Oaks
Reading and Fine Arts Instructor
Columbus City Schools
Columbus, Ohio

Elizabeth Shupe
ABE/ESL Instructor
Right to Read of Weld County
Greeley, Colorado

Erma Thomspon
Developmental Studies Instructor
Dallas, Texas

Gail Rice
Palos Alto, Illinois

Rita Milios
Toledo, Ohio

Christina Hutzelman
Kettering, Ohio

Reviewers

Mary Jo Balistreri
ABE Coordinator, Adult Education
Fairfield Career Center
Carroll, Ohio

Connie J. Dodd
ABE Instructor
Frontier Central School District
Hamburg, New York

Julie Gerson
Coordinator
Goodwill Literacy Institute
Pittsburgh, Pennsylvania

Dr. Patricia Kuhel
English/Reading Specialist
Labette Community College
Parsons, Kansas

Laura Weidner, Director
Applied Technology and Apprenticeship
Catonsville Community College
Catonsville, Maryland

Table of Contents

Nutrition, Health, and Safety

Workplace Skills

The Reading Corner

Posttest for Book 4 . . . .**115**

Name _____ Pretest for Book 4

A. Put a √ next to the words with the same **g sound** as the first word.

    1. **engine**   a. _____ gate   b. _____ giant   c. _____ charge

    2. **guess**   a. _____ arrange b. _____ golden c. _____ gather

B. Put a √ next to the words with the same **c sound** as the first word.

    3. **cave**   a. _____ cart   b. _____ city   c. _____ curtain

    4. **cabin**   a. _____ juice b. _____ country c. _____ captain

C. Put a √ next to the synonym for the first word.

    5. **filled**   a. _____ empty b. _____ stuffed

    6. **start**   a. _____ end   b. _____ begin

D. Put a √ next to the antonym for the first word.

    7. **noisy**   a. _____ quiet b. _____ sounds

    8. **sit**   a. _____ recline b. _____ stand

E. Circle the two words that sound the same but have different meanings in each line below.

9. for	of	four	far
10. it	I	elf	eye
11. sent	sign	cent	sea
12. knows	know	nose	now

F. Add a prefix to the following words to give them the opposite meanings.

    13. afraid _____   14. fill _____

G. Put a √ next to the best answer.

15. Maria went to the _____ to wash her clothes.

    a. _____ store   b. _____ laundry c. _____ supermarket

16. The children sang a _____ to their mother for her birthday.

    a. _____ present b. _____ party   c. _____ song

H. Read the story. Put a √ next to your answer.

Do you get colds? Did you know that almost everyone gets a cold? Some people get at least two colds a year. How do you feel when you have a cold? You may have a sore throat. You may sneeze. Your nose may be stuffed or it may run. You may also have a bad cough. Picture yourself with watery eyes and a fever. This is not a pretty picture. A less pretty thought is that there is no known cure for the common cold.

17. What was the story mostly about?

    a. _____ being sick with a cold

    b. _____ pretty pictures

    c. _____ the common cold

18. The sentence in the story that says, "Your nose may be stuffed or it may run," means

    a. _____ you cannot breathe well from your nose and you probably need a handkerchief.

    b. _____ your nose wants to run away.

    c. _____ your nose drips.

I. Put a √ next to the meaning for the underlined word in the sentence.

19. I like orange juice for breakfast

    a. _____ a fruit   b. _____ a color

20. She was very patient with the little girl.

    a. _____ a sick person   b. _____ willing to wait

A Letter From School

Read what the teacher's letter asked David's mother and father to do.

A Letter From School

Marta's son David came home from school and gave his mother a letter. It was from his teacher, Ms. Chang. The letter asked Marta to call her. Marta didn't know why the teacher wanted to talk to her.

David had been in kindergarten for two months and was doing well in school. Marta thought, if the teacher wants to talk to me, maybe David isn't doing well.

Looking for Answers

Marta asked David some **questions** about school. She asked him if he liked school, his teacher, and the other children. David told her he did like school, his teacher, and most of the other children.

Marta asked her husband, Pedro, to go with her to talk to Ms. Chang.

Pedro told his wife, "My dad didn't talk to my teachers, and I don't need to talk to David's teacher."

questions *things that people ask*

Marta asked Pedro, "Isn't David important to you? Don't you care how he does in school?"

"Yes," said Pedro, "but I don't know what to say to the teacher."

"I will go talk to my friend Helena," Marta said. "Her children have gone to school for many years. She will know how to talk to the teacher."

A Talk With Helena

"Did you get a letter from Ms. Chang?" Marta asked her friend.

"Yes," said Helena. "I am going to meet her Monday at 2:00 P.M."

"Have the children done something **wrong**?" asked Marta.

"Oh no," Helena said, "it's called a **parent-teacher conference**. It is very important. You will learn how David is doing in school, and you can ask the teacher some questions."

"What will the teacher say?" Marta asked Helena.

"She will ask if you have any questions about David."

"What should I ask her?"

"You might ask if David gets along with the other children or ask what you can do at home to help him."

Then Helena said, "Before you go, ask David if he has any questions. Ask him what he likes and doesn't like about school. You may want to tell Ms. Chang some things about David."

Feeling Better

Marta went home and told Pedro what Helena had said.

"Pedro, now I want to talk with Ms. Chang," said Marta. "Helena told me this is a conference with the teacher. It is very important. It isn't easy the first time, but it gets easier the next time. Helena said she has talked to teachers many times."

Marta looked at her husband and smiled. "She said David

wrong *not right*

parent-teacher conference *a school meeting between a child's teacher and his or her parents*

didn't do anything wrong. We should ask David some questions before we go, and then we can ask the teacher some questions, too. We will know what David is learning and find out if we should help him at home. I feel better now, Pedro. Will you go with me to the conference?" Marta asked her husband.

"OK, I will go."

"Can you go Tuesday at 5:00 P.M.?" Marta asked.

"Yes," Pedro answered.

Marta called Ms. Chang and told her they were coming.

The Parent–Teacher Conference

Marta and Pedro went to David's school. They knew it was important to be on time. When they went into David's classroom, Ms. Chang said, "Hello, I'm glad you are here. Sit down, please."

Ms. Chang told Marta and Pedro that David was a good boy. "He plays well with the other children. His handwriting is getting better. He likes to work with numbers and colors."

Ms. Chang showed David's work to Pedro and Marta.

"Do you have any questions for me?" asked Ms. Chang.

Marta wanted to know, "How can we help David?"

"Well," Ms. Chang said, "do you know that David doesn't know your first names? I would like him to know how to write his address. Are these things you could help David with?"

"Oh, yes," Marta and Pedro said at the same time.

Ms. Chang asked some questions. "Do you read books to David? Do you listen to him read to you? Does David see you reading?"

"Is this important?" Marta asked.

"Yes," answered Ms. Chang. "If David knows you read to learn things, he will want to learn that way, too."

Pedro said, "I will read with David when I get home from work."

"David and I will read when he gets home from school," said Marta.

Marta and Pedro thanked Ms. Chang for her time.

"I am so happy you came to learn about David. He is lucky his mother and father think school is important. You are his first teachers, and together we can help David. Please call me if you have questions. I am glad David is in my class this year."

After the Parent–Teacher Conference

Pedro is happy he went with Marta. Now he knows what David does every day. He knows how important school is and how he can help David. They will work together every day. Pedro thinks David will be a good **student**.

student *a person in school*

Marta is happy she went to talk to Ms. Chang. Now she knows what David is learning. Pedro and I will help him learn more, and he will be a good student, Marta thinks. Next time it will be easier to talk to Ms. Chang. I must go talk to Helena and thank her for her help. Now David will know we think school is important.

Words, Words, Words

A. A **contraction** is a short way to write two words. The word *couldn't* is a contraction. It takes the place of the words *could not*. The (') is used with a contraction. It stands in for the missing letters. In *couldn't* the (') stands for the letter **o** in *not*. Here are some contractions. Write the words they stand for. Then, use each contraction in a sentence. The first one is done for you.

1. isn't __is not   She isn't in school today._____

2. doesn't _____

3. didn't _____

4. I'm _____

5. they're _____

B. The words *Marta's son* show that the son belongs to Marta. Look at the **'s**. It is used to show that something belongs to a person or a thing. Read the words below. Use the **'s**. The first one is done for you.

1. the teacher of David __David's teacher_____

2. the friend of Marta _____

3. the book that belongs to Pedro _____

4. the classroom of David _____

5. the child of Helena _____

6. the car that Steve owns _____

7. the letter from school _____

Word Story:

The word burro *is a Spanish word. It means "a small donkey." A burro is sometimes used as a pack animal. Have you ever seen a burro?*

C. The following words have short vowel sounds: **a** in *cat,* **e** in *pet,* **i** in *pin,* **o** in *cot,* and **u** in *tub.* Complete each sentence with the short vowel sound word. The first one is done for you.

1. Do you (know, have) any answers? _____**have**_____

2. Marta feels (better, good). _____

3. David likes the children in his (group, class). _____

4. Pedro is Marta's (husband, neighbor). _____

5. How can we (help, pay) David? _____

D. Sometimes two letters together stand for one sound. Look at the pairs of letters below. Together they make one sound. Use the best pair of letters to make a word in each sentence. The first one is done for you.

sc   ck   wr

1. David is a lu__**ck**__y boy.

2. His hand_____iting is better.

3. Marta goes ba_____ home.

4. Did David do something _____ong?

5. The teacher will che_____ his answers.

6. He likes art. He learned to use _____issors with care.

E. Use the following words in a sentence.

1. conference _____

_____

2. wrong _____

_____

3. address _____

_____

4. kindergarten _____

_____

Understanding

A. A **fact** is something that you know is true. An **opinion** is what you feel or believe.

Marta has a friend named Helena. This is a fact.

Helena is the best friend in the world. This is an opinion.

Write **F** if the sentence is a fact. Write **O** if the sentence is an opinion. The first one is done for you.

1. __F__ David likes school.

2. _____ Ms. Chang is a good teacher.

3. _____ Helena is Marta's friend.

4. _____ David likes to work with numbers.

5. _____ Marta is a good parent.

6. _____ Pedro goes to the conference.

7. _____ School is important to Marta and Pedro.

8. _____ David is in kindergarten.

B. Read the sentences below. Find the best endings for them. Put a √ next to your answer.

1. Next time Marta talks to the teacher it will be

   a. _____ about Pedro.   b. _____ at her home.

   c. _____ tomorrow.   d. _____ easier.

2. Pedro will help David

   a. _____ clean his room.   b. _____ ride a bike.

   c. _____ with his school work. d. _____ tie his shoes.

Discussion

A. What are some ways that you could help a child in school? Use the web below to show these ways. Fill in the empty circles.

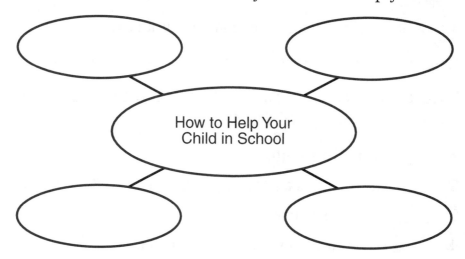

How to Help Your Child in School

B. Write an answer to each question below. Think about what could happen because of the choices people make.

1. Pedro and Marta think school is important. How will they let David know?

_____

_____

_____

2. Marta talked to her friend Helena. How did their talk help Marta?

_____

_____

_____

LESSON 2

Reading Aloud

Learn why reading aloud to children is important for them.

Why Read Aloud?

Most parents want to know what they can do to help their children do well in school. Reading aloud to children is one of the best things a parent can do to help them read and learn.

Some children do not do well in school because they have a hard time sitting still and listening. Reading aloud helps children become better listeners. It helps them to listen for a longer time.

Hearing stories read aloud also helps them begin to read. They begin to learn the sounds of letters. They start to learn many new words.

Reading to children helps them to want to read on their own. They will learn to love reading and books.

Children who read learn how words are used. They learn to speak well. They are able to talk about their ideas and thoughts clearly. Using words the right way will not be a hard thing for them to do.

Children who read have fewer problems learning to write. Unlike watching TV, hearing a story helps children use their minds. Children can "see" in their minds. They can see people, places, and things in the story. Doing this helps them to think about things that are new to them. It also helps them use their **imagination** when they make up their own stories.

imagination an active mind

There is another reason to read to children. Spending time with children helps them to feel good about themselves. They will feel special because you have spent time with them. They will feel closer to you. You will have fun together. You will have the books to talk about.

Loving books as a child will carry over into adult life. People who read will have a way to bring fun and learning into their lives forever. They, too, will pass this love of books on to their children. Books help children get interested in many things. One thing might be a **hobby**.

hobby a favorite thing to do

When Should a Child Start Reading?

It is never too early to start reading to a child. Some parents start reading when they get their baby home from the hospital. Others start to read aloud when the baby can hold his or her head up and look at the pages in a book.

Children at this young age learn very quickly. Babies love the sound of their mothers' and fathers' voices. Reading to babies makes them feel **content**. Start to read to them when children are young. As they get older, they will probably ask you to read to them again and again.

content being happy or feeling OK

Is It Ever Too Late?

It is never too late to start reading to a child. Older children enjoy hearing good stories. They may want to read part of the book to you. Older children will enjoy talking about the books, so let them ask questions. Be sure to read books about the things they like. There are many books written about sports, games, **heroes**, and other fun things.

Much older children may like to watch a lot of TV or play TV games. They may have school work or team **practice** that leaves them little time for reading. They may think reading is for babies. Remember that reading to children will help their minds. Be **patient** and don't give up. Read little things to them from the newspaper. The sports page, the funny page, or the movie ads might interest them.

heroes *very brave people*

practice *do again and again*

patient *willing to wait*

What Do You Read?

Picture books are good books for babies because they like to look at colorful pictures. They will learn many words when you name different things. For example, a picture of a farmyard can help them learn the names of colors, the names of animals, the parts of animals' bodies, and words like *big, little, tall,* and *short.*

Making the sounds of the different animals as you name them can be fun for babies. Reading short stories is also good for them. They like hearing your voice while you hold them.

For young children, short stories are best to hold their interest. Choose books about things they like. Children like to look at pictures in books. Of course, books don't have to have pictures. Children can use their minds to "see" the things you read about.

Some adults choose books that will teach children about people, places, or things. They pick books that will help children learn about life. They pick books that teach lessons such as telling the truth, being kind, or helping others.

How Do You Find the Time?

Bedtime is a good time to read to children. Most children like having their parents close by as they fall asleep.

You can read to a child almost anywhere. Read aloud while the child is bathing, waiting with you in the doctor's office, or riding on the bus. At mealtime you might read the **cereal** box. While shopping you can read the cans or boxes of food. The child will learn to put the pictures with the words. Read the road signs and the billboards.

Try to find time to read whenever or wherever you can.

cereal *a food from grain*

Reading Tips

1. Read in front of children. It is important for them to see you read.

2. Have books in the house. Keep books where children can see them.

3. Limit the time that children watch TV.

4. Talk to children about the books you read.

5. Not all children can sit still. It's OK if they move around while you read.

6. Go to the library with children.

7. Put reading to children *first*. Dirty dishes can wait.

8. Practice reading the book before you read aloud to children.

9. Read with feeling but don't overdo it.

10. Pick books that you and the children will enjoy.

Words, Words, Words

A. Read each pair of words below. Some are antonyms. Some are synonyms. **Antonyms** are words with the opposite or almost opposite meaning. **Synonyms** are words that mean the same or about the same thing. On each line, write **A** for *antonym* or **S** for *synonym*. The first two are done for you.

1. hot ___A___ cold

2. job ___S___ work

3. talk _____ speak

4. early _____ late

5. sad _____ happy

6. short _____ long

7. buy _____ sell

8. love _____ hate

9. house _____ home

10. happy _____ glad

B. A **compound word** is a word made from two words. For example: *daytime* is a compound word made from the words *day* and *time*. Write on the lines the two words that make the compound words. The first one is done for you.

1. whenever   __when__   __ever__

2. bedtime   _____   _____

3. another   _____   _____

4. storytime   _____   _____

Read the story again. Find one or two compound words. Write them on the lines.

5. _____   _____

6. _____   _____

Word Story:

The word tortilla *is a Spanish word. It means "a thin disk of bread made from cornmeal or flour." It is served with beans, meat, or cheese. Have you ever eaten a tortilla?*

C. Some words have long vowel sounds. Listen to the **long a** in *snake*, the **long e** in *heat*, the **long i** in *drive*, the **long o** in *open*, and the **long u** in *tube*. Complete each sentence with a long vowel sound word. Write your answer on the line. The first one is done for you.

1. His (cape, hat) was blue. __**cape**_____

2. Connie likes to have a (plum, donut) for a snack. _____

3. (We, They) are good friends. _____

4. Would you like to (pet, meet) my new puppy? _____

5. The boys (wake, get) up early every morning. _____

6. Sue left her (pen, paper) at home. _____

7. Dave saw the pretty (cat, cake) at the store. _____

8. The (jet, jeep) makes noise. _____

D. The letters **th** and **ch** in a word can stand for one sound. Read the sentences. Use **th** or **ch** to complete the words. Make sure the word fits the meaning of the sentence. The first one is done for you.

1. Kate wrote a ___**ch**__eck at the bank.

2. Bess and Neil have only one _____ild.

3. I am older _____an you.

4. They go to _____ur_____ every Sunday.

5. She wants to be _____in like her sister.

6. George is looking for a _____eap car to buy.

7. Joel is in the _____ird grade.

8. Read the story and _____en answer the questions.

9. _____ew your food so you won't _____oke.

Understanding

A. Read the questions below. Use the story to help you give your answers.

   1. What do you think might be different about children who are read to and children who are not read to?

      _____

      _____

   2. What is different about reading to a young child and reading to an older child?

      _____

      _____

B. Read the sentences below. Find the best endings for them. Use the story to help you. Put a √ next to your answer.

   1. Children who are read to will

      a. _____ become good readers.

      b. _____ earn a lot of money.

      c. _____ write their own books.

   2. If children see others reading,

      a. _____ they will think the TV is broken.

      b. _____ they will also want to read.

      c. _____ they will feel lonely.

Discussion

A. Read the questions below. Use the story to help you give each answer.

1. When is it a good time to start reading to children?

   _____

   _____

2. What kinds of books are good for children?

   _____

   _____

B. A **fact** is something you know is true. An **opinion** is what you feel or believe.

There are books written about people. This is a fact.

Hero stories are the best type of stories. This is an opinion.

Write **F** if the sentence is a fact from the story. Write **O** if the sentence is an opinion.

1. _____ All children like to read.

2. _____ Girls read more than boys do.

3. _____ You need a library card to take books from the library.

4. _____ Stories about sports are better for boys.

5. _____ All homes in the U.S.A. have TV sets.

6. _____ Only parents should read to their children.

A Closer Look at the Dictionary

A dictionary is a helpful book. You can use it to learn about words. You can learn

- how words are spelled,
- what words mean and,
- how to say words.

To learn about words, you must be able to find them in a dictionary. A dictionary is easy to use! All the words are listed in **A-B-C,** or **alphabetical**, order. Words beginning with the letter *a* are all together. The words beginning with the letter *b* are in their own group, and so on.

At the top of each dictionary page you will see two **guide words.** Guide words help you to know what words are on that page. The guide word on the left is the first word on the page. The guide word on the right is the last word on that page. The page number is in the middle. The words between the guide words are in alphabetical order.

Look below. This is how guide words look on a dictionary page.

blood   25   **blow**

The guide words **blood** and **blow** are also in alphabetical order. The first three letters of both words are *blo.*

What is the fourth letter of blood? It is the letter *o*. What is the fourth letter of blow? It is the letter *w*. Remember that the letter *o* comes before the letter *w* in the alphabet. This is why the word *blood* comes before the word *blow* on page 25 of this dictionary.

A. Look at the words below. Study the letters in each word. Would you find them on page 25 of this dictionary? Answer Yes or No.

1. bloom _____   2. blot _____

3. blue _____   4. bluff _____

5. blouse _____   6. blend _____

B. Look at the words below. Write them in the order you would find them on a dictionary page.

meat   meets   mat   metal   match   matter   meant   meal

1. _____   2. _____

3. _____   4. _____

5. _____   6. _____

7. _____   8. _____

C. Answer the questions below. Use your own words and ideas. Use a dictionary.

1. What is the purpose of guide words? _____

_____

_____

_____

2. Name some things you can learn about words from a dictionary.

_____

_____

_____

LESSON 3

Arlene

FAMILY LIFE

Read about a teenager who helps her family.

Arlene's Family

Arlene Nestor's mother was very sick. Sometimes her mother had to stay in bed all day. On these days, Arlene took care of her.

Arlene also had a little sister, Sonya. Sonya was only four years old. She also needed someone to take care of her. Arlene looked after her, too.

When her mother was sick, Arlene was sad and afraid. She couldn't go to school. She was in her last year in high school. Arlene wanted to learn. She didn't like to miss days. She went to school as often as she could.

Arlene was a good student. She learned quickly. She liked to read and to study. She also liked to be with her friends at school. They laughed together and had fun.

Arlene at Home

When her mother was not feeling well, Arlene had many things to do at home. Arlene cooked the food and cleaned the house. She washed the clothes and put them away. Sometimes Arlene played with Sonya and read books to her. Sonya liked for Arlene to read to her. When she had time, Arlene read books and newspapers for herself.

skills *ways
to do things*

wisely *knowing
about*

Numbers were easy for Arlene. She liked math. She could add and subtract. These **skills** helped when she had to buy food and other things for her family. When her mother was well, she went shopping with Arlene. She had taught Arlene how to buy **wisely**. When Arlene went shopping alone, she did not spend too much. She knew her family didn't have a lot of money. They needed money to pay the bills. They needed money to pay for the doctor and the medicine.

Arlene's Mother

Arlene's mom became sicker. She became very quiet and didn't want to eat. She could not get out of bed without help. The doctor told Arlene it would be a long time before her mother got better. Arlene and Sonya were very sad to hear this.

Sonya

Arlene stayed home from school more and more. She had many things to do at home. Sonya wanted Arlene to spend more time with her. She wanted someone to do things her mother once did with her. She wanted Arlene to tuck her in bed at night and read stories to her. She needed someone

to spend lots of time with her. She was just a little girl who felt **scared**. She didn't like it that her mother was sick.

scared *afraid*

Soon Arlene stopped going to school at all. She spent her days caring for Sonya and their mother. Arlene missed school and her teachers and friends. She missed the fun.

Mrs. Brown

The family had a nice **neighbor**. Her name was Mrs. Brown. She lived alone. She helped Arlene's family. She brought soup or homemade bread for them to eat. She helped Arlene do the work. Sometimes she stayed with Sonya and Mrs. Nestor while Arlene went to the store.

neighbor *someone who lives nearby*

Things Get Better

As the months went by, Mrs. Nestor started to feel better. She could sit up more and more. She would eat the soup Mrs. Brown brought in the evening. She spent more time with Sonya. She told her girls how much she loved them and how **proud** she was of them.

proud *happy or pleased with*

One day Arlene read in the newspaper about a class for people who wanted to finish high school. People could get a high school **equivalency diploma** if they studied and passed the GED tests. They could go to classes a few hours a day. When the teachers said they were ready, they could take a test. The test was called a GED test. If people made a good grade on the test, they would get their high school equivalency diploma.

equivalency *equal in value*

diploma *a paper showing completed studies*

Arlene was excited! She told her mother and Mrs. Brown she wanted to go to these classes. Mrs. Brown said she would stay with Sonya and their mother while Arlene **attended** classes.

attended *was there*

The Classes

Arlene liked the classes and her teachers. She liked the other people in the classes, too. She learned very quickly. She listened to the teachers and took **notes**. She wanted to pass the GED tests. She wanted her high school equivalency diploma.

notes *written-down information*

Sometimes Arlene talked about her lessons with her mother. Her mother was happy for Arlene. She was feeling better each day.

A Special Dinner

It took a long time for Mrs. Nestor to get better. But one day she was well enough to make a special dinner for her family and Mrs. Brown. It was a dinner for Arlene. She had passed the GED. Arlene now had her high school equivalency diploma.

Moving On

Arlene's mother continued to get better each day. She often told her girls how proud she was of them.

Little Sonya started school and was learning to read. She came home every day with a fun story to tell her mother and sister. She was happy again.

Mrs. Brown still helped them when they needed someone. She was part of the Nestor family now.

succeeded *turned out OK*

Arlene got a good job working at a store close to their home. She liked her job. It had not been easy for a young girl to take care of the family, but Arlene had **succeeded**. When Arlene remembered the times her mother was so sick, she felt proud of the way she had taken care of things. She was glad that she had gone to the GED classes. She had learned a lot. Now she had her high school equivalency diploma. She could help Sonya with her lessons now. It was easy to smile now. She was happy again.

Words, Words, Words

A. A **contraction** is a short way to write two words. The word *didn't* is a contraction. It takes the place of the words *did not*. The (') is used with a contraction. It stands in for the missing letters. In *didn't* the (') stands in for the letter **o** in *not*. Here are some contractions. Write them next to the words they mean.

aren't   isn't   couldn't   they're   you're

1. could not _____

2. you are _____

3. is not _____

4. are not _____

5. they are _____

Word Story:

Hamburger *is a word that was first used in Germany. The people of Hamburg, Germany, used to eat pounded beefsteak. Americans started calling it* hamburger *in 1902.*

B. In some words, two letters together can stand for one sound. Look at the pairs of letters below. Write the best pairs to finish the words.

sc   ck   wr

1. Arlene's mother was si_____.

2. Mrs. Brown _____ote the note.

3. The lunch was in the sa_____.

4. Sonya learned to _____ite her name.

5. She learned qui_____ly.

6. Arlene showed Sonya how to use _____issors.

C. The vowels are *a, e, i, o,* and *u*. The following words have **long vowel sounds: a** in *bake,* **e** in *beat,* **i** in *drive,* **o** in *open,* and **u** in *tube*. Complete each sentence with the long vowel sound word.

1. Matt likes to eat (cake, apples). _____

2. Jane will (beat, bless) the egg. _____

3. Connie walked on the (ice, hill). _____

4. He will (go, mop) over the floor. _____

5. The (tube, tub) is empty. _____

6. We need to (rake, pack) the leaves. _____

7. Kris likes to (write, fix) stories. _____

8. Alice has (three, ten) dollars to spend. _____

D. Underline the two words that sound the same but have different meanings in each line. The first one is done for you.

1. <u>bee</u>	bees	best	<u>be</u>
2. four	of	for	far
3. new	no	knew	knee
4. know	knows	now	nose
5. two	toes	too	tow
6. flood	floor	flower	flour
7. sun	soon	son	seen
8. at	eight	night	ate
9. send	sum	sent	some
10. blew	blow	blue	flow

Understanding

A. A **fact** is something you know is true.

A week has seven days. This is a fact.

An **opinion** is what you believe or feel.

Sunday is the best day of the week. This is an opinion.

Write **F** if the sentence is a fact from the story. Write **O** if the sentence is an opinion.

1. _____ Arlene wanted to learn.

2. _____ Sonya was always a nice little sister.

3. _____ Mrs. Brown helped Arlene and her family.

4. _____ Arlene liked being with her friends.

5. _____ Mrs. Brown lived next door to the Nestor family.

6. _____ Sonya liked to eat soup.

7. _____ Mrs. Nestor said she was proud of her girls.

8. _____ Sonya was the best reader in her class.

B. Read the sentences. Find the best endings for them.
Put a √ next to your answer.

1. Arlene

a. _____ wanted to learn.   b. _____ didn't want to learn.

2. Mrs. Brown was

a. _____ a good neighbor.   b. _____ a bad neighbor.

3. Sonya was Arlene's

a. _____ cousin.   b. _____ sister.

Discussion

A. Use the story to help you give the answers.

   1. Why did Sonya need someone to take care of her?

   _____

   2. Who taught Arlene how to buy wisely?

   _____

   3. How did Arlene find out about the classes?

   _____

B. What are some ways Arlene learned? Use the web below to show these ways.

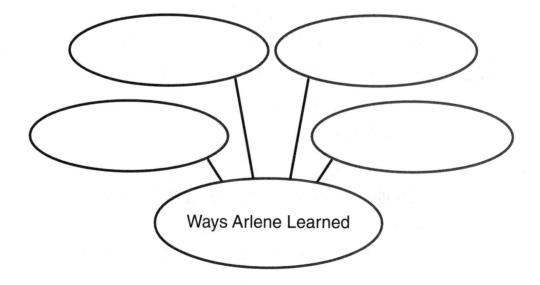

Ways Arlene Learned

Luka

Read about Luka and her cakes.

FAMILY LIFE

Luka Petroni

Luka pulled the cord for the bus driver to stop at the next corner. She walked to the front exit door, carefully carrying a large cake box. It held her special white icing cake.

"Goodnight, Mr. Gomez." Luka smiled at the driver. He was an old friend. He had driven this bus **route** ever since Luka was a little girl.

route *way or road*

"Watch your step, Luka. That cake of yours made my bus smell like pure heaven. I wouldn't want you to drop it."

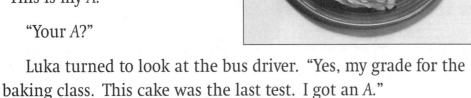

"No way," Luka laughed as she stepped down to the curb. "This is my *A*."

"Your *A*?"

Luka turned to look at the bus driver. "Yes, my grade for the baking class. This cake was the last test. I got an *A*."

"Well, good for you. See you soon." Mr. Gomez closed the bus doors and drove away.

Luka's Neighborhood

Luka walked along the street carefully carrying her cake box. She had lived in this neighborhood all her life and knew every crack in the sidewalk. She wasn't going straight home tonight. Home was a nice big apartment she shared with her mother and Gran. They knew she planned a stop tonight so they wouldn't be holding dinner.

Mr. Schmidt's Bakery

destination *a place someone is trying to reach*

Luka took a deep breath as she drew closer to her **destination**. She was going to Mr. Schmidt's bakery. She passed his store every day. When she was a little girl, she had bought cookies from him with her pennies. Her mother bought fresh bread from him every morning. Before her hands got stiff, her Gran had decorated cakes for him whenever there were rush orders.

dessert *food served at the end of a meal*

events *happenings*

decorations *writing, flowers, or designs on a cake*

Mr. Schmidt was known all over the city for his cakes. They were served for **dessert** at many important city **events**. People ordered them months ahead of time. It was the icings and **decorations** that made them so special. His bread and cookies were also in great demand.

Luka stood outside the closed bakery, but she knew Mr. Schmidt was in the back working. He was waiting for her and had told her just to ring the bell when she got there.

The front of the store was softly lit, but Luka could see the glass cases that were empty now. All the sweets and breads were sold or stored away for tomorrow.

A Hope

Luka could also see the cardboard sign taped to the window. It had been there for the past two weeks. It read:

> **HELPER WANTED**
> To Bake and Decorate Cakes
> ASK INSIDE

She wanted to be that helper. She knew she could be a cake decorator. NO! not *could be* . . . she *was* a cake decorator. She wanted to own a store like Mr. Schmidt's. She wanted people to know about her cakes and to order them for birthdays and weddings. She had worked very hard for this kind of chance.

Gran Petroni

Luka's Gran had also been a cake decorator in her **homeland**. She brought **recipes** and skills that had been passed down from mother to daughter. Gran was not a young woman anymore. Her hands were **stiff** and sore. She could not decorate her cakes.

Luka's father was her son. He had died when Luka was just a little baby. Gran had tried to teach her daughter-in-law, Luka's mother, to decorate cakes, but she did not have the skills. It was Luka who had stood beside Gran at the kitchen table. She had watched and learned. Luka listened to Gran and, in time, began to do her own baking.

Gran had shared all her secrets with Luka. Now Luka knew the recipes and had the skill to decorate cakes.

Luka knew from her mother and Gran that it was important to have other skills. She needed to know math and reading. How could she **measure** or write and read recipes? So Luka worked hard in school. She had her high school diploma. She was also taking baking classes at the neighborhood center. She wanted to take part-time classes at the community college.

White Icing

The special cake Luka was now carrying was from her last class. The white icing was her very own recipe. She thought it

homeland *your own country; the country where you were born*

recipes *cooking directions*

stiff *hard to bend*

measure *to find the right amount*

was her best. The teacher and the class thought so also. She had had to bake two cakes. She decorated both of them. One was for show. The other was used for the taste test. She had received an *A* for each cake. She felt very proud. She felt ready to meet with Mr. Schmidt.

The Meeting

apprentice
someone who learns a job from another person

Mr. Schmidt wasn't surprised when Luka told him she wanted the job. If he liked her cake, she could become his **apprentice**. She could go to school and work for him on her free days. He would teach her more about being a great cake decorator.

Luka rang the bell. Before she knew it, Mr. Schmidt opened the door. "Come in, Luka. I've been waiting for you. Let's see your cake."

Mr. Schmidt cut the string and carefully lifted the cover. "Oh my! Luka, your cake looks like a dream. If it tastes as good as it looks, you will be my apprentice."

Three Years Later

Everyone stood in the kitchen smiling at Luka. Luka's mother wiped tears from her eyes.

"Best wishes, Luka," Mr. Gomez said.

"I am so proud of you, my dear girl," Gran said and hugged Luka.

Luka had finished school. She took business classes along with baking classes. Besides baking, she now knew many things about running a business. This was her party. Her cakes were becoming as well known as Mr. Schmidt's. She even had an order for the mayor's birthday cake.

"Come, everyone. Have a slice of this cake. This is one of the finest cakes Luka has made yet," Mr. Schmidt said and smiled at his new partner.

Words, Words, Words

A. Read each pair of words. On the line write **A** for **antonym** or **S** for **synonym**.

1. big _____ small

2. end _____ final

3. bad _____ good

4. go _____ stop

5. fast _____ slow

6. hard _____ soft

7. full _____ empty

8. happenings _____ events

9. near _____ far

10. sad _____ happy

Word Story:

You might use shampoo to wash your hair. Did you know the word shampoo *is a word from Hindi? It means a "liquid to clean the hair or scalp."*

B. There are words that sound alike but do not look the same or mean the same thing. For example:

The word *one* means a number. He has *one* sister.

The word *won* means to win. The team *won* the game.

Write the right word to complete the sentence on each line.

1. He drove the same (root, route) for many years. _____

2. How much does the box (way, weigh)? _____

3. She (knew, new) everyone who lived in the neighborhood. _____

4. They made dinner (four, for) her. _____

5. She (red, read) the sign. _____

6. Her hands were stiff and (sore, soar). _____

7. She (maid, made) many cakes. _____

C. Some words have **long o** or **long u** vowel sounds.
Words like *home, rope, use,* and *mule* all have long vowel sounds.
Read the words below. Put a √ next to the words with **long o**
or **long u** vowel sounds.

1. _____ tube   2. _____ drop   3. _____ hut

4. _____ robe   5. _____ stove   6. _____ tune

7. _____ hung   8. _____ zone   9. _____ luck

10. _____ pole   11. _____ fuse   12. _____ wrote

D. The letter **g** has different sounds. It can have a soft sound
if it is followed by *e, i,* or *y,* as in the word *large.* It can have a
hard sound if it is followed by other letters, as in *gold.* Write
the word on the line to complete each sentence based on the
g sound. The first two are done for you.

1. Hard g sound
   The box was in the (cage, garden). _____ garden _____

2. Soft g sound
   The story was about a (goose, giant). _____ giant _____

3. Hard g sound
   The (gate, engine) made a funny sound. _____

4. Soft g sound
   The (game, page) was lost. _____

5. Hard g sound
   He drew a picture of a (gun, giraffe). _____

6. Soft g sound
   There were many (germs, geese) in the air. _____

7. Hard g sound
   The (goat, judge) drank the milk. _____

Understanding

A. Read the questions below. Use the story to help you give each answer.

1. Why did Luka want people to know about her cakes?

_____

_____

2. What do you think the last words in the story mean? "Mr. Schmidt said and smiled at his new partner."

_____

_____

3. Why do you think Luka's mother was crying at the party?

_____

_____

B. Read the questions below. Think about what happened in the story. Use the story and your own ideas to answer the questions.

1. What do you think Luka will do next?

_____

_____

2. What do you think Mr. Schmidt will do next?

_____

_____

Discussion

A. Answer the questions below. Use the story to help you give the answers.

1. Who thought Luka's white icing cake smelled wonderful? _____

2. What time of the day did this story take place? _____

3. Who taught Luka to bake and decorate? _____

4. Where was Luka's father? _____

5. What grade did Luka get for her white icing cake? _____

6. Who was known all over the city for his cakes? _____

7. What kind of classes did Luka take? _____

8. What is an apprentice? _____

B. **Summary.** This word means to tell something again in a short way. In your own words tell what you read in the part of the story called **"Gran Petroni."**

_____

_____

_____

_____

_____

_____

You Can
Tell What's Happening

Pictures can tell stories without using any words. The picture below tells its own story. Study the picture to find out what story it tells. Then, answer the questions on the next page.

A. Use the picture to help you answer these questions.

    1. Where do you think the picture was taken?

_____

_____

2. What time of year is it? _____

_____

3. How many people are in the picture?

_____

4. What are they doing? _____

5. How do the people look? (happy, sad, or afraid) Tell why you think this.

_____

_____

_____

B. Now, write a story about what is happening in the picture. There are many things to write about. Tell about the boy and the man. Give them names. Tell what they are talking about. Remember that it's your story.

_____

_____

_____

_____

_____

_____

_____

_____

Renting an Apartment

Anita and Rob are a young couple just starting out.
They want to find a nice apartment to rent.

Time to Move

Rob had a job when he and Anita got married. Anita did not have a job. The young couple decided to live with Anita's mother until Anita found a job.

Anita was **eager** to find a job. She and Rob wanted a place of their own. In two months, Anita found a good job. She became an **aide** at a day care center. She liked the job from the start.

eager *to really want to do something*

aide *a helper*

The day came when Anita received her first paycheck. She and Rob now knew how much money they would have each month. That evening they started to look for an apartment.

Getting Started

"In what part of town should we look?" Rob asked. "The newspaper ads seem to **divide** the city into five areas."

divide *to cut into parts*

"With one car, it would be good for us to be on the bus line," said Anita. "I'll get the city map."

Anita unfolded the large yellow map on the table. She and Rob sat next to each other and smiled.

"This should be fun, Rob. Just think about how we can fix up a place we'll call home."

"It will be fun, but we have a lot of work to do. Now, here's the day care center. Here's the repair shop," Rob said as he marked the map with a red pen. "We both work close to Clark Street, which has buses running on it every 15 minutes."

"Yes. So, we can live in this east area," Anita said pointing to the map. "Then, either one of us could take the bus. Are there many ads for that part of town? And, how much is rent in that area? We can only pay about $400 per month for rent." Anita sounded worried.

"Don't worry, honey. There are plenty of apartments for rent." Rob gave Anita a hug. "Let's see what we can find in these ads."

Looking at Ads

Reading together, Anita and Rob saw two ads that mentioned Clark Street. They marked them.

> **APARTMENT FOR RENT:** unfurn 2 BR, 1 bath,
> off Clark, electric heat, water incl.,
> coin op w/d in building, no pets, dep. required.
> $435/mo. Call 425-6700 eves.

> **APARTMENT FOR RENT:** unfurn 1 BR, 1 bath,
> near park on Clark and Fifth, ac., pets OK,
> dep. required. $390/mo. Call Joe 425-8156 eves.

"Well, Anita, these two places sound good. The two-bedroom is a little more money. Do you think we should look at the one-bedroom apartment first?"

"I'd sure like an extra room," Anita said. "We could have a small desk in there where you could do the paperwork from the repair shop. And, we could put a bed in there so my sister could visit."

"Let's call these numbers, Anita. We may like one better than the other after seeing them both."

"I want to read the leases carefully, too," added Anita. "We need to know what is in each lease before deciding which apartment to rent."

"You're right. Some landlords are **strict**. We need to know what we're getting into." Rob began to dial the first number. "We are on our way, Anita," he said with a big smile. "Soon, we'll have a HOME, SWEET HOME sign over our door."

strict *follow rules carefully*

Seeing Each Apartment

The next evening Anita and Rob visited the apartments they found in the newspaper. They took a checklist of things to look for in each place and questions to ask each manager:

_____ Try every water faucet. Any leaks?

_____ Flush the toilet. Any problems with plumbing?

_____ Does stove work? Does refrigerator work?

_____ Clean? Freshly painted? Any sign of bugs?

_____ What about storage?

_____ Is the area noisy? Is it safe?

_____ May we see the lease? How much is the **security deposit**?

security deposit *money given to hold something*

Making a Decision

Finally, Anita and Rob were ready to decide. They read each lease carefully and went through their checklists.

"I really like the two-bedroom place," said Rob, "but the lease says we can't **sublet**. If we don't like the apartment and want to move in a few months, we will owe a lot of money."

"The security deposit there is a full month's rent. We'd have to wait another month for my next paycheck to be able to pay the deposit and the rent," Anita said with concern.

sublet *to rent to another for a short amount of time in the lease*

"Well, the apartment near the park has a month-to-month lease. So, we could move at any time without extra cost if we wanted."

"I liked that one, too, Rob. It seemed clean and was very quiet. And, the security deposit was only $200. We can afford that now."

budget *a plan for how much money you need and can spend*

"Also, the rent fits right into our **budget**," Rob said happily.

"We'll just put a desk in the bedroom for your work and a pull-out sofa in the living room for company." Anita was seeing the apartment in her mind.

"What do you think, Anita? We don't want someone else to rent our home, do we?" Rob laughed.

"Whoa! Let's read the lease for that place one more time, Rob. Then, if it still seems OK, we'll call the landlord."

Reading the lease again, Anita and Rob decided the apartment near the park was right for them. Anita grinned as she dialed their future landlord's number. She and Rob were soon to have a place of their own.

42

Words, Words, Words

A. A **prefix** is a group of letters added to the beginning of a word. They will change the meaning of the word. **Re-** and **un-** are prefixes.

> **re-** means "again"
> **un-** means "not"

heat   Mother will reheat the soup.
             Reheat means *to heat again.*

safe   The old bridge was unsafe to drive across.
             Unsafe means *not safe.*

Add **re-** or **un-** to the words below. Then use one of the new words in a sentence.

1. read _____

2. clean_____

3. known _____

B. Writers try to use words that give a strong feeling. These words help you, the reader, to understand and enjoy the story. Read the sentences below.

a. The wind blew against the door.
b. The cold, frosty wind hit hard against the door.

Which sentence gives you a stronger feeling? Did you say *b*? Put a √ next to the sentences below with the stronger feeling. The first one is done for you.

Word Story:

Do you use ketchup on your hamburger? The word ketchup, *sometimes spelled* catsup, *is a Chinese word. It means "a smooth sauce made from tomatoes."*

1. a. ____ Linda was cold as she walked through the snow.

   b. _√_ Linda shivered as she plodded through the snow.

2. a. ____ The rain hit against Larry's face.

   b. ____ The icy rain stung Larry's face.

3. a. ____ Tom's boss talked to the group in a loud voice.

   b. ____ Tom's boss shouted angrily at the group.

4. a. ____ The kitten hid under the old table.

   b. ____ The fluffy kitten crouched under the wobbly table.

5. a. ____ Sue strolled through the bright, colorful garden.

   b. ____ Sue walked through the plant store.

C. Some words have the letters **ee** and **ea**. These letters sometimes have the sounds you hear in the words *eat, free, seed,* or *breeze*. The sound you hear is the **long e sound**. Use **ee** or **ea** to finish each word. The first two are done for you.

1. Josie will be fift___**ee**___n years old in May.

2. The m___**ea**___t will cook for two hours.

3. I had to wait for a s_____t on the bus.

4. The window scr_____n was torn by the cat.

5. Our football team b_____t the number-one team.

6. I had to scr_____m over the noise of his music.

7. Pl_____se hand me the bottle of milk.

D. Sometimes two consonants together stand for one sound. The pairs of letters **wr, kn, sc, ck,** or **gn** together make one sound. Make a word in each sentence using one of these pairs.

1. He did not si_____ the papers.

2. Do you have the key to the lo_____?

3. My grandmother likes to paint pretty _____enes.

4. Who is _____ocking at the door?

5. She gave Sam the _____ong phone number.

6. Rob will che_____ the window lock.

7. Do you _____ow their neighborhood?

Understanding

A. Write **F** if the sentences below are facts from the story. Write **O** if the sentences are opinions.

1. _____ Anita's mother is a nice person.

2. _____ Anita and Rob have one car.

3. _____ Anita and Rob are married.

4. _____ Rob is a good worker.

5. _____ Rent for Anita and Rob's apartment is $390.

6. _____ The apartment near the park is the better apartment.

7. _____ Anita works at a day care center.

8. _____ Rob had a job when he and Anita got married.

9. _____ Anita and Rob could only pay $400 per month for rent.

B. Do you think Anita and Rob made a good decision to rent the one-bedroom apartment? Give reasons for your answer.

_____

_____

_____

_____

_____

_____

Discussion

A. What are the main ideas for the following parts of the story? Put a √ next to your answer.

1. **Time to Move**

   a. _____ Anita is looking for a job.

   b. _____ Anita and Rob would like to find an apartment.

   c. _____ Anita's mother helped the young couple.

2. **Getting Started**

   a. _____ Rob likes to read the newspaper.

   b. _____ The city has a good bus service.

   c. _____ Anita and Rob try to decide which area of town to live in.

B. Read the questions below. Use the story to help you give each answer.

1. Why did Anita and Rob want to find an apartment?

   _____

2. Why did they want a place on the bus line?

   _____

3. Why did the young couple want to read the leases?

   _____

4. Why did they decide to rent the one-bedroom apartment?

   _____

A Closer Look at a Lease

Read Anita and Rob's lease below. Answer the questions that follow.

LEASE AGREEMENT

1. In agreement are __Leroy Cane__ called "Landlord," and __Rob Sims and Anita Sims__, called "Tenant," for property located at __143 Lake Boulevard, Apt. C__.

2. The term of this rental agreement shall be for __month-to-month__, beginning on __Aug. 1, 2000__ and ending on __one month's notice by tenant__.

3. The monthly rental for said property shall be $ __390__ due on __first day__ of each month.

4. Utilities shall be paid by party listed below:

   Electricity __Tenant__   Gas __Tenant__

   Water __Landlord__   Other __None__

5. Tenant agrees to:
   a. Keep dwelling clean and sanitary; repair damage caused by Tenant at his/her own cost or be liable to Landlord for reasonable expense to Landlord for said repair.
   b. No alteration of property without prior consent of Landlord.

c. No excessive noise or other activity that disturbs the peace.

6. Landlord agrees to:

a. Enter Tenant's property only with Tenant's prior consent unless Landlord believes an emergency situation exists or is inspecting the property for possible violation of this agreement.

b. Repair property (damage not due to Tenant's violation) within reasonable period of time upon notice of need from Tenant at no cost to Tenant.

7. The Tenant shall pay Landlord upon signing a security deposit of $__200__. This deposit may be used by the Landlord for any cost due to Tenant's violation. Unused deposit will be returned to Tenant within two weeks of leaving the apartment.

A. Use the lease to answer the questions below.

1. When is the rent due? _____

2. What must Anita and Rob do when they decide to move out of the apartment? _____

3. What utilities must Anita and Rob pay? _____

4. Anita's three-year-old nephew wrote on the living room wall during a visit. Rob repainted the room. Who pays for the paint? _____

5. Rob would like to put another cupboard in the kitchen. What must he do before he begins? _____

6. In October, Anita found a large leak under the bathroom sink. What should she have done about it? _____

7. What was the amount of the security deposit? _____

8. In December, Anita and Rob's car needed to be repaired. As a result of this expense, they do not have their whole rental payment for January. What should they do?

_____

_____

LESSON 6

The Iron

Beth and Carol are old friends. Now they share their first apartment.

What to Buy?

Beth and Carol had many choices to make about their new apartment. What should they buy? Could they pay for a TV, VCR, or CD player? They decided they could **afford** only a CD Boom Box. They bought used furniture from the Salvation Army and Goodwill stores. The sofa, chairs, tables, and lamps looked nice in their apartment.

afford *to have enough money to buy something*

Buying an Iron

They needed an iron. They wanted one that would shut off by itself. It would be safer in case they forgot to turn it off. They went to the Amos **Catalog Store** to buy the iron. The catalog told about each shut-off iron. They read about each iron.

catalog store *a store that lists in a book the things it has to sell*

> **Light and Easy Shut-Off Iron**
> Shuts off in 15 minutes
> 4 steam settings • Lightweight
> 2-year **warranty** • $24.00

> **Deluxe Shut-Off Iron**
> Shuts off in 10 minutes or in 30 seconds if tipped
> On/off/ready light • 6 steam settings
> Mist spray • Self-cleaning with Silver Stone coating
> 2-year warranty • $38.00

warranty *a written promise a company gives to a buyer for certain repairs to a product such as a TV or an iron*

> **Ultra 55 Shut-Off Iron**
> Shuts off in 10 minutes
> Off/on/ready light • 6 steam settings
> Self-cleaning • No-drip steam spray
> Fabric guide • 2-year warranty • $50.00

A Warranty

The warranty was the same for each iron. Each iron would be fixed if it didn't work. The warranties were good for two years. The irons had to be used correctly or the warranty would not be good.

Beth and Carol had to be careful with the iron. They also had to follow the directions for the iron they chose. If they didn't, the iron wouldn't be fixed for free if it broke. All repair work had to be done at the Service Center.

Making a Choice

They decided that $50.00 was too much to spend. They chose the Deluxe Shut-Off Iron. The price fit their budget. The easy ironing coating was important. Carol filled out the order form. She gave it to the salesclerk. He told them to keep their **receipt** and the warranty in a safe place. They might need them later.

At their apartment, they read the directions for the iron. They filled out the warranty **registration card**. They put the receipt and the warranty in a file box where they kept paperwork for everything they bought. They mailed the card to the company that made the iron. Now the warranty was filed with the company.

Using the Iron

The iron was great. The steam and the coating made it easy to iron. Beth and Carol were always careful when they used it. But three months later, even with their care, the iron wouldn't get hot. Carol turned it on and nothing happened. She checked the plug and the ON setting again, but the iron just didn't get hot.

"Beth, the iron won't heat up!"

receipt *a paper that shows you bought something and how much you paid for it*

registration card *a card that comes with a product such as an iron, a TV, or a CD player. When mailed into the company, the item is recorded for any later repairs.*

50

"You're kidding! Did you check the directions?"

"No, but I will," replied Carol.

Carol checked the directions for the iron. She read the part about **troubleshooting**. She had done everything correctly, but the iron would not get hot. The directions said to call the 800 Service Number.

Before Carol called, she found the receipt for the iron in the file box. She dialed 1-800-555-4321.

troubleshooting *directions on how to solve problems with an item such as an iron, a mixer, a TV, or a CD player*

Getting Help

An **operator** answered and asked, "How may I help you?"

Carol answered, "Our iron won't get hot."

"What is the name and model of the iron?" the operator asked.

Carol said, "The Deluxe Shut-Off Iron, Model XB332."

operator *a person who answers the phone for a company*

"When and where did you buy the iron?"

"It was on August 24 at the Amos Catalog Store."

The operator said, "Your iron is still under warranty. You can take it to one of our Service Centers. It will be fixed for free. What is your ZIP Code?"

Carol gave the operator her ZIP Code.

"The Service Center in your area is at 222 Broad Street. Take your receipt and your iron to that Center. Thank you for choosing our iron."

Carol and Beth took the iron to the Service Center the next day. The repair person asked what was wrong with the iron. They told her the iron would not get hot.

"Let me take a look. I'm sure it can be fixed. It should be ready in three days. I'll need your name, address, telephone number, and where you bought the iron. May I also see your receipt?"

"Beth, do you have it?" asked Carol.

"Oh no! I thought you brought it."

"I'm sorry, but I can't fix the iron without the receipt."

"I'll come back with it later today. What time do you close?" asked Beth.

"We close at 6 P.M."

"I'll be back before then," said Beth.

Results

Beth brought the receipt to the Service Center. She received a copy of the work order. That night she put the receipt and the work order back into the file box.

Three days later the Service Center called to say the iron was fixed.

Beth went and took both the work order and receipt with her. She gave the work order to the repair person who showed Beth that the iron was fixed.

Beth and Carol never had any more trouble with the iron.

Words, Words, Words

A. **Antonyms** are words that have opposite meanings, such as *heavy* and *light* or *fast* and *slow*. Put a √ next to the word that has the opposite meaning from the first word in each line.

1. buy   a. ____ bought   b. ____ sell

2. fix   a. ____ break   b. ____ repair

3. keep   a. ____ save   b. ____ lose

4. safe   a. ____ secure   b. ____ unsafe

5. remember   a. ____ forget   b. ____ know

B. Read the sentences below. Put a √ next to the word or words that match the meaning of the underlined word.

1. Beth and Carol needed to keep receipts for everything they <u>bought</u>.

   a. ____ found   b. ____ wanted   c. ____ purchased

2. Their budget showed them what they could <u>afford</u>.

   a. ____ able to pay for   b. ____ need   c. ____ want

3. When the iron wouldn't work, Carol read the <u>directions</u>.

   a. ____ warranty   b. ____ instructions   c. ____ price

4. They sent the registration card to the <u>company</u>.

   a. ___ catalog store   b. ___ Service Center   c. ___ manufacturer

Word Story:

A mattress is a soft material to sleep on. In Arabia some people sleep on lots of pillows thrown on the floor. The word mattress *comes from the Arabic word* matrah, *meaning "a place where something is thrown."*

C. Vowels can have a **short sound** as in *hat, get, it, hot,* and *just.*
They can also have a **long sound** as in *made, me, light, home,*
and *rude.* Read the sentences below. Write **S** for a **short sound**
or **L** for a **long sound** for the underlined word. The first one is
done for you.

1. They mailed the registration <u>card</u>. _____**S**_____

2. The repair person needed their <u>ZIP</u> Code. _____

3. The <u>iron</u> would not get hot. _____

4. They bought a <u>nice</u> iron. _____

5. The iron was <u>fixed</u>. _____

D. The letter **c** has two different sounds. It can sound like **k** in
the word *cash* or like **s** in the word *nice.* Read the sentences
below. Write **k** or **s** for the **c sounds** in the underlined words.

1. They went to a <u>catalog</u> store. _____

2. The Service <u>Center</u> was nearby. _____

3. They filled out the registration <u>card</u>. _____

4. The sales <u>clerk</u> gave Beth the iron. _____

5. The <u>receipt</u> was in the desk. _____

E. The letter **g** has two different sounds. It can sound like **g** in
the word *go* or **j** in the word *large.* Look at the words below.
Write **g** or **j** for the **g sounds**.

1. registration ____   2. forgot ____

3. good ____   4. gentleman ____

5. catalog ____   6. great ____

7. giant ____   8. garden ____

9. game ____   10. general ____

Understanding

A. Beth and Carol made many decisions. Use the story and your ideas to answer the questions below.

1. Why did Beth and Carol buy furniture from the Salvation Army and Goodwill stores?

   _____

2. They bought a shut-off iron for safety. Name two other safety items people buy.

   _____

3. Name two safe places to keep important papers.

   _____

4. Beth and Carol were careful about the money they spent. Write an idea you have that can save money.

   _____

   _____

B. Write your answers using the story to help you.

1. List things that were the same about the irons in the Catalog Store.

   _____

2. List things that were different about the irons in the Catalog Store.

   _____

Discussion

A. This story gives many ideas. If the sentences below match what you think is one of the ideas in this story, write **Y** for *Yes*. If they do not match, write **N** for *No*.

1. _____ It is not important to plan ahead for what you want to buy.

2. _____ It is important to follow directions.

3. _____ It is a good thing to keep important papers in a safe place.

B. Beth and Carol were given directions to follow about the iron and its use. Write one direction given to them from the people listed below.

1. Salesclerk

   _____

   _____

2. Operator

   _____

   _____

3. Repair person

   _____

   _____

You Can
Follow Directions

Anita and Rob live a few miles from their jobs. One morning, their car wouldn't start. So, Anita and Rob both had to take the bus to and from work. They had a bus schedule for the route near their apartment. They live on Lake Boulevard (Blvd.). Use the bus schedule on the next page to answer the questions below.

1. What is the route number for this bus schedule? _____

   _____

2. Rob's workplace is off Poplar Road. Where should Rob wait for the bus in the morning? He lives on Lake Blvd. _____

3. What direction, north or south, is Rob going to get to work? _____

4. Rob needs to be at work by 8:30 A.M. When should he be at his Bus Stop #3? _____

5. Anita works on Clark Street near St. Luke's Hospital. Where should she wait for the bus? _____

6. Anita needs to be at her job by 7:00 A.M. What time should she be at her bus stop? _____

7. What stop is best for Anita to get off the bus?

   _____

8. Rob gets off work at 5:00 P.M. What time should he be at his bus stop to get home? _____

9. At what bus stop does Rob get off the bus to get home after work? _____

_____

10. If Anita finishes work around 3:00 p.m., how long will she wait before going home by bus? _____

Bus Schedules

NORTH
MONDAY — FRIDAY

① CLARK ST. & POPLAR RD.	② CLARK ST. & COMO ST.	④ CLARK ST. & RED RD.
7:25 a.m.	7:30 a.m.	7:45 a.m.
8:15 a.m.	8:20 a.m.	8:35 a.m.
1:15 p.m.	1:20 p.m.	1:35 p.m.
4:25 p.m.	4:30 p.m.	4:45 p.m.
5:15 p.m.	5:20 p.m.	5:35 p.m.

SOUTH
MONDAY — FRIDAY

④ CLARK ST. & RED RD.	③ CLARK ST. & ROBIN AVE.	① CLARK ST. & POPLAR RD.
6:30 a.m.	6:35 a.m.	6:45 a.m.
8:00 a.m.	8:05 a.m.	8:15 a.m.
12:05 p.m.	12:10 p.m.	12:20 p.m.
5:00 p.m.	5:05 p.m.	5:15 p.m.

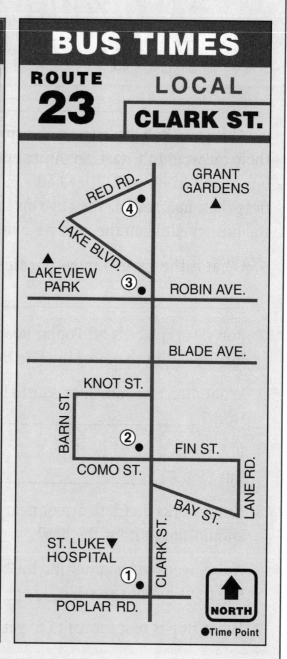

BUS TIMES

ROUTE 23 **LOCAL** **CLARK ST.**

GRANT GARDENS ▲
RED RD.
④
LAKE BLVD.
▲ LAKEVIEW PARK
③ ROBIN AVE.
BLADE AVE.
KNOT ST.
BARN ST.
② FIN ST.
COMO ST.
LANE RD.
BAY ST.
ST. LUKE ▼ HOSPITAL
CLARK ST.
① POPLAR RD.

▲ **NORTH**
● Time Point

LESSON 7

Baby Safety Rules

NUTRITION · HEALTH AND SAFETY

Read how hospitals keep new babies safe.

The First Rule—ID Bracelets

Dr. Joan Morgan looked at Sue. Then she looked at Sue's husband, Joe. The doctor's face broke into a grin a mile wide. Dr. Morgan said, "It's a girl!"

Sue heard her baby's cry. Her face lit up like a Christmas tree. The nurse took the baby over to a table where other nurses waited. They washed her little body. They put a warm hat on her head. Then one of them got out a blanket. Before they wrapped her up, they did something very important. They put an **ID** band on her arm.

An ID band is sometimes called an ID **bracelet**. It is made of a strip of flat, soft **plastic.** Usually it is about a half-inch wide and long enough to go around a baby's wrist. Often it is white. It looks like a tiny bracelet.

ID bands usually have a number printed on them. They also have blank areas where nurses write things with an ink pen. Usually they write the baby's name, weight, and birthdate. They also write the mother's name and if the baby is a boy or a girl. Sometimes they write the name of the baby's doctor.

ID *a paper or badge showing who a person is*

bracelet *a band worn on the arm or wrist*

plastic *material that can be easily shaped*

The nurse put the ID band on the baby. Then she put a band on Sue's arm and one on Joe's arm. The number on their bands was the same number as the one on their baby's band. The bands were all the same and showed that this baby was theirs.

It seemed strange to Sue that before she was allowed to hold her baby, they all had to have bands put on. Later she asked the nurse about this.

The nurse said, "The first thing we do is put ID bands on the baby and his or her parents. Then if anything happens or the baby needs to be taken out of the room, everyone is marked."

Sue and Joe wore the bands until the baby went home. They were given strict orders not to take them off. The nurses looked at these bands many times. They looked at Sue's band when they brought her baby to her room. They looked at Joe's band when he picked up the baby from the nursery. They always made sure the baby's band matched the parents' bands. The nurses were very careful.

The Second Rule—
Teach Parents the Hospital Rules

staff *a group of workers*

prevent *stop from happening*

Checking bands was only one thing the hospital **staff** did to keep babies safe. They also taught all parents the hospital's Baby Safety rules. There are two reasons for these rules. The first is to **prevent** babies from being stolen from the hospital. The second is to keep babies from being given to the wrong parents.

Baby Safety rules were made for very important reasons. So, everyone has to follow the rules. Doctors, nurses, parents, and visitors have to follow all the rules all the time. This is the only way to make sure the babies are safe during the time they are in the hospital.

There are many hospitals in the United States. Some are small. Some are as big as a city. Some are in towns. Some are in the country. They are all different. Most of them have Baby Safety rules. However, each hospital decides on its own rules.

The Third Rule—Name Badges

Sue and Joe's baby was born in a hospital in Ohio. This hospital had a rule about name **badges**. Everyone who worked at the hospital had to wear a hospital name badge all the time. The badges had the name of the hospital, the staff member's name, and a picture.

badges *name pins that are worn to be seen by others*

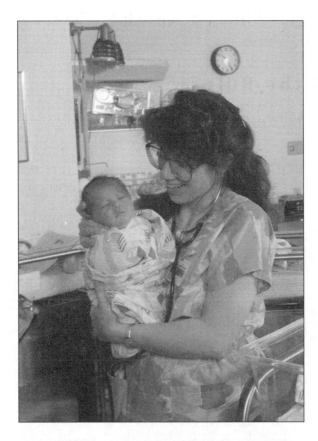

Sue's nurse told her to always look for the hospital badge and never let anyone who wasn't wearing a hospital badge take the baby. Sue had to look for the badge whenever her baby was taken from her. Even if someone was dressed like a nurse or a doctor, she was to look for the badge. Sue's nurse was very strict about this rule. Sue was very careful, too. She always looked for the badge.

The Fourth Rule—
Never Leave Them Alone

The hospital had another rule. Babies could not be left alone. When Sue took a bath, she had to call a nurse. The nurse came to the room and took the baby back to the nursery. If Sue took a nap, she would call the nurse to take the baby to the nursery. When she was done with her nap or bath, the nurse would bring back the baby.

Why All the Rules?

Nurses and doctors have new parents follow many rules. At times the rules are hard to remember. Sometimes they are not easy to follow, but these rules were made for one reason—to keep babies safe.

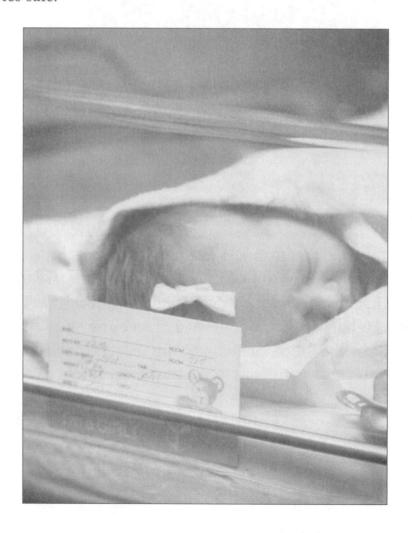

Words, Words, Words

A. Read the sentences below. They are from the story "Baby Safety Rules." Now read the two sentences that follow. Put a √ next to the sentence that tells what the line means in the story.

1. The doctor's face broke into a grin a mile wide.

    a. _____ The doctor had a very wide face.

    b. _____ The doctor had a big smile.

2. Her face lit up like a Christmas tree.

    a. _____ A light was shining on her face.

    b. _____ She had a very happy look on her face.

B. **Compound words** are two words together that make a new word. For example: the words *cup* and *cake* together make the new word *cupcake*. The word *blanket* is not a compound word. The word *blank* is a word but the letters *et* do not make a word. Read the words below. Put a √ next to the compound words.

1. ____ daytime
2. ____ payroll
3. ____ showed
4. ____ bylaw
5. ____ birthday
6. ____ tracing
7. ____ waited
8. ____ margin
9. ____ carryout
10. ____ pocketbook
11. ____ wallet
12. ____ market
13. ____ bracelet
14. ____ keyboard
15. ____ number

Word Story:

At the zoo you may have seen an alligator. This large reptile lives in swamps in hot areas. The word alligator *comes from the Spanish word* el lagarto, *which means "the lizard."*

Now, write the compound words as two words. The first one is done for you.

16. cupcake   __cup__   __cake__
17. paperwork   _____   _____
18. basketball   _____   _____
19. handbook   _____   _____
20. bookstore   _____   _____

C. The letters **ay** and **ai** usually stand for the **long a sound** as in *play* and *train*. Read the sentences below. On the line, write the word or words that have the **long a sound** in each sentence.

1. The nurse waited by the cart. _____

2. Her husband stayed with her. _____

3. Sue took a nap during the day. _____

4. Joe didn't want it to rain. _____

5. The nurse covered Sue with a gray blanket. _____

D. Sometimes, two consonants together stand for one sound. The pairs of consonants **gn, sc, wr,** and **kn** together make one sound. Write the best pair of letters on each line. Make sure the word fits the sentence.

1. The nurse will _____ite her name on the band.

2. Dr. Morgan liked _____ience in school.

3. Joe fell and hurt his _____ee.

4. Sue wore the band on her _____ist.

5. Joe brought flowers. They had a nice _____ent.

6. Sue _____ew the name of the hospital.

7. Kecia read the si_____ on the door.

8. Stan desi_____ed the new hospital.

9. She will _____it the baby a warm hat.

10. Dr. Morgan _____ote a note to the nurse.

Understanding

A. Read the sentences. Find the best ending for them.
Put a √ next to your answer.

1. As soon as a baby is born in a hospital, the nurses

   a. _____ have a party.
   b. _____ wash the baby and wrap the baby in a blanket.
   c. _____ leave the room and take a coffee break.

2. Baby Safety rules are important because

   a. _____ they help keep babies safe.
   b. _____ they give the doctors something more to think about.
   c. _____ they help the hospitals make money.

3. A woman came into Sue's room. She told Sue she was taking the baby to the nursery. Sue first

   a. _____ handed the baby to the woman.
   b. _____ called for help.
   c. _____ looked for an ID badge.

B. Read the questions below. Write your answers on the lines.

1. Sue, Joe, and their baby wore ID bands. What was the same about the bands? _____

   _____

2. Many people worked at the hospital. What one thing did they have to wear to follow a hospital rule? _____

   _____

Discussion

A. Read each question below. Use the story to help you give an answer.

1. Name the four Baby Safety rules given in the story.

   a. _____

   b. _____

   c. _____

   d. _____

2. In what state was Sue and Joe's baby born?

   _____

3. What did the nurse tell Sue to look for if someone came to take the baby?

   _____

4. Where did the nurse take the baby when Sue took her nap?

   _____

5. Why do hospitals have so many rules about babies?

   _____

B. In your own words, tell two things hospitals can do to keep babies safe.

   1. _____

   _____

   2. _____

   _____

You Can
Solve the Problem

Every day you solve problems. Some problems are easy to solve. Should I do my shopping now or later? Some problems are harder. My car is in the shop. How will I get to work? Some problems change a life forever. Can I afford to go to school?

Every day life brings problems and choices. The kinds of choices you make can make your life easier or harder. Things may go right or wrong. Often, you do not know which way they will go. But there are ways to help you be surer. There are steps you can take. You can look at your choices before you make a decision. You can see some of the problems you may face. You may see that you have other or better choices.

Here are some steps to help you solve problems.

Step 1   Know what the problem really is. Is it a daily problem? Is it a once-in-a-lifetime problem?

Step 2   List the things you know about the problem. List the things you don't know. Ask questions. Get help and advice.

Step 3   Write down your other choices.

Step 4   Think about a good and a bad for the other choices. Put them in order from best to worst.

Step 5   Pick the choice you feel good about.

Step 6   See what happens after you make your choice. Are you happy about the choice? Would you make it again?

Read the story below:

Sue has cancer. Her doctor told her that it is only in one place in her body. The doctor wants to operate on Sue's cancer. He thinks that will take all of it away. But he still wants Sue to do something else. He wants her to take medicine for four months. The medicine will make her feel very sick. It will make her tired. But the medicine can help keep the cancer from coming back.

Sue is not sure what to do. She has two small children who are not in school. Sue's husband works days and cannot help care for the children during the day. Sue's family lives far away. She cannot afford day care. She asks herself, "How will I be able to care for my children if I am sick?"

The doctor told Sue that she must make her own choice. Will she take the medicine? Sue must decide. She will talk with her husband. They will make a choice together.

Your Turn to Help

What is Sue's problem? What are her choices? What would you decide? Write in the steps below that help you make a choice:

Step 1   The problem is _____

Is it a daily problem or a once-in-a-lifetime problem? _____

_____

Step 2   a. You know these things about the problem: _____

_____

b. You don't know these things about the problem: _____

_____

Step 3   The other choices are: _____

_____

Step 4   Rank the choices, best to worst _____

_____

Step 5   Pick a choice the family might feel good about. _____

_____

Step 6   What might happen to Sue and her family? _____

_____

Diabetes and You

Read about diabetes.

What Is Diabetes?

Diabetes is a **disease**. Many people have diabetes. You or someone you know might have diabetes. Every day doctors tell 1,700 more people that they have this disease. Some people have diabetes and do not know it.

Diabetes was once called "sugar diabetes." Some people still say, "I have sugar in my blood." Or they say, "I have sugar." Doctors call this blood sugar **glucose**.

What Does Diabetes Do?

Diabetes makes many changes in your body. The biggest change is that your body no longer uses food for energy in the same way. Usually when you eat, your body makes energy from sugar and **starch** in your food. Your body changes this sugar and starch into blood sugar. Then this blood sugar flows through your blood to all parts of your body.

At the same time, something else happens. The body also makes insulin. It flows through the blood with the blood sugar. Since your body can't use all the glucose at the same time,

disease *a problem in your body that makes you sick and causes your body not to work right*

glucose *sometimes called* blood sugar; *the sugar you eat turns into this once it is in your blood; it gives you energy*

starch *something found in foods like potatoes or noodles and used by the body the same way it uses sugar*

insulin *something found in your body that is needed to help change blood sugar into energy*

insulin tells the body how much glucose to use. It tells the body when to use more and when to use less. You need more blood sugar when you work hard. You need less when you rest.

If you have diabetes, your body does not make enough insulin. The insulin cannot keep up with all the blood sugar it has to change. Sometimes your body may not make any insulin at all. Either way, your blood sugar does not get used up fast enough. You have "high sugar."

High blood sugar causes many problems. You may have to go to the bathroom a lot. You may eat a lot and still lose weight. You may feel weak and tired. It may become hard for you to see. Cuts or sores may take too long to heal. These things can cause other problems later on.

Who Gets Diabetes?

Anyone can get diabetes. Men and women can get it. Children can get it. People who are overweight can get diabetes easier. Women get diabetes more often than men. Women who have very large babies (bigger than ten pounds) get it easier.

Age also plays a part in diabetes. Older people (over 65) get it more often. As your body ages, it may not work as well. Sometimes insulin is harder to make. Then diabetes can start.

Few children get diabetes. Less than ten percent of people with diabetes are children. When children get diabetes, it is a real problem. The loss of insulin is greater. Many children with diabetes have very little insulin. Some have none at all, so they have a greater need for extra insulin.

Some people with diabetes must take shots to put extra insulin into their bodies. Adults usually don't need the shots for a long time. Children usually need them right away.

Types of Diabetes

Because diabetes works in different ways, it has different names. Type I Diabetes is the kind children get. It must be watched closely by a doctor. The child has to take shots of insulin each day. Children with Type I Diabetes must check their blood every day. They prick their finger with a special pin. Taking a small drop of blood, they place it on a special testing strip that is used with a special testing machine. The machine shows a number that tells the amount of blood sugar. The number must be in a certain **range**. If it is too high or too low, there are certain things that have to be done.

Sometimes children also check their **urine**. To get urine to check, they go to the bathroom in a cup. They test their urine on a special paper. The paper changes color. The color is matched against a **chart**. The colors on the chart show if everything is in a **normal** range. The color can also show if there is a problem with the blood sugar.

With Type II Diabetes, you do not need shots. Type II Diabetes can be cared for with a special diet and exercise. A doctor tells you what to eat. He tells you how much to exercise. He tells you the range your blood sugar should be in when it is tested.

With diet and exercise, you can keep your blood sugar in a normal range. You can't eat sweet foods or drinks. You must eat

range *a group of numbers that have a beginning and end*

urine *body water that comes out when you go to the bathroom*

chart *a paper which lists numbers, letters, or colors and gives information*

normal *the way things should be*

certain **amounts** of different types of foods—fruits, meats, breads, vegetables, and fats. With less sugar in your food, there is less sugar in your blood. You should then have enough insulin. It can take care of your blood sugar.

Things to Remember About Diabetes

Type II Diabetes starts slowly. It causes problems that may be hard to see at first. It is important to watch for these signs:

- Families often have more than one person with diabetes. So if one family member has diabetes, it is important for other family members to watch for it.

- As you get older or are over the age of 65, you must watch more carefully.

- If you are overweight, you are more at risk.

- If you are a woman who had a large baby, you are also more at risk.

If you have diabetes, it is important to listen to your doctor. Eat right and exercise right. Get lots of sleep and rest. If you do these things, you can live well with diabetes.

Words, Words, Words

A. Read the sentences below. Use the sentences to find out what the underlined words mean. Put a √ next to the best meaning.

1. You do not feel well when you have a <u>disease</u>.

   a. _____ something that makes you sick

   b. _____ something that makes you mad

2. There are <u>warning</u> signs that tell you if you have diabetes.

   a. _____ something to try to do

   b. _____ something to watch out for

3. Your body uses blood sugar for <u>energy</u>.

   a. _____ to give power

   b. _____ to perform daily tasks

4. Some people with diabetes must get a <u>shot</u> every day.

   a. _____ a hit from a gun

   b. _____ a stick with a needle

5. Type II Diabetes can be cared for with a special diet and <u>excercise</u>.

   a. _____ body movement

   b. _____ discussion questions

B. Put a √ next to the word or words in each line that sound alike but have different meanings.

1. a. ____ two   b. ____ too   c. ____ tow   d. ____ to

2. a. ____ some   b. ____ sun   c. ____ sum   d. ____ soon

3. a. ____ do   b. ____ doe   c. ____ due   d. ____ dew

4. a. ____ for   b. ____ far   c. ____ four   d. ____ fork

Now write a sentence for each word you put a √ next to in line 3.

_____

_____

_____

_____

C. The letter **y** can stand for the **long e sound** as in the word *party*. The letter **y** can also sound like the letter **i** as in the word *try*. Read the words below. Write **e** or **i** on the line to tell the sound of **y** in each word.

1. body ____   2. my ____   3. heavy ____   4. baby ____

5. dry ____   6. candy ____   7. really ____   8. fly ____

D. The pairs of letters **kn, wr,** and **ck** can make one sound. Use these pairs of letters to make a word in each sentence. Make sure the words fit the sentences.

1. She did not _____ow she had diabetes.

2. To test your blood, you can pri_____ your finger with a special pin.

3. She went ba_____ to the doctor for a test.

4. A doctor may _____ite a list of things you need to do.

Understanding

A. Sometimes you can tell what a writer is thinking by the way he or she writes a sentence. Read the sentences from the story. See if you can tell what the writer was thinking. Put a √ next to your answer.

1. Many people have diabetes. Every day doctors tell 1,700 more people they have diabetes.

   a. ____ The writer thinks diabetes is a big problem.

   b. ____ The writer thinks diabetes isn't a big problem.

2. Some people still say, "I have sugar in my blood." What they really mean is they have diabetes.

   a. ____ The writer thinks everyone knows diabetes is "sugar in the blood."

   b. ____ The writer thinks some people may not know diabetes is "sugar in the blood."

3. The writer says, "Women who have big babies may get diabetes."

   a. ____ The writer thinks a "big" baby means one who weighs over ten pounds.

   b. ____ The writer thinks a baby over ten pounds is small.

B. Read the sentences below. If the sentence is a fact from the story, write **F.** If it is an opinion, write **O.**

1. ____ Diabetes is an illness.

2. ____ Diabetes is the worst illness you can get.

3. ____ People with diabetes eat too much candy.

4. ____ Cuts that don't heal could be a sign of diabetes.

Discussion

A. Read the questions below. Use the story to help you with your answers.

1. Type II Diabetes is different from Type I. Why?

_____

_____

2. How does age play a part in Type II Diabetes?

_____

_____

3. Some people are more likely to get diabetes than others. Who are they?

_____

_____

B. Which of the following best describes the whole story?
Put a √ next to your answer. Choose 1 or 2.

1. ____ Diabetes is an illness. Many people get it. There are two kinds of diabetes. These are Type I and Type II. You can look for the warning signs of diabetes. If you get diabetes, diet and exercise may help. But some people need to take shots. It is important to ask your doctor about diabetes.

2. ____ Diabetes is an illness. It is also called "sugar in the blood." With diabetes, the body does not use sugar for energy as it should. Too much sugar stays in the blood. That is why it is called "sugar in the blood."

LESSON 9

NUTRITION · HEALTH AND SAFETY

Roy Lives With Diabetes

Each year many people find out that they have diabetes. Roy is one of these people. Read how he learns to live with his diabetes.

Roy Sees a Problem

Roy woke up in the middle of the night. "Oh, good grief!" he said. "I have to go to the bathroom again. Maybe it's because I drank too much water last night. But lately, I'm always **thirsty**."

The alarm clock rang the next morning. Roy could barely get up. Even though he had gone to bed early the night before, he was still very tired this morning.

"How did you sleep?" his wife, Millie, asked.

"Not so good," Roy answered. "I'm still getting up three or four times during the night to go to the bathroom."

"I told you, Roy, to go to the health center. Your Uncle Sam had the same problem. The doctor told him that he had a disease. He had to go on a special **diet**. I think he got shots for it, too, but that was after he had had it for a while."

thirsty *needing a drink of water*

diet *a special food plan*

"Yes, I remember," said Roy.

"Well, dear, maybe you have what Sam had. You must find out. That's the only way you can get better." Millie held his hand in hers. "I don't want anything to happen to you, Roy."

"I know, Millie. I'll call the doctor today."

"Good. Everything will be OK, Roy," said Millie.

At the Doctor's Office

Later that week, Roy sat on Dr. Bell's table. The doctor asked him a lot of questions and he looked at a cut on Roy's arm.

"Roy," he said, "I think your wife may be right. I think you may have diabetes. I am going to do another test to be sure. The nurse will tell you about it. You will have to come back another day. Here are some papers about diabetes that you should read. Write down any questions. Bring them with you the next time. We will talk then."

"OK, doctor." Roy looked unhappy.

Dr. Bell looked carefully at Roy. "Don't worry, Roy. You can live well with diabetes. You will have to change your eating **habits**. Give up sweets. Pay more attention to what and when you eat." The doctor looked at Roy's **stomach**. "You also need to go on a diet."

"Oh, no! You mean I can't eat Millie's apple pie anymore?"

"No," said Dr. Bell. "I'm sorry."

Talking With Millie

At home, Roy talked with Millie about what the doctor had said. They read the papers about diabetes.

"This paper called 'The Warning Signs of Diabetes' sounds like you, Roy," Millie said. "But at least your diabetes can be helped with diet. Do you think you will have to take shots, too?"

habits *the way people do things*

stomach *the body's food sac*

"I don't know," answered Roy. "I'll have to ask Dr. Bell."

Millie looked worried. Roy put his arm around his wife. "It'll be OK," he said. But he couldn't look into Millie's eyes. He didn't want her to see his tears.

Roy Thinks About Diabetes

"Blast it! Why did this have to happen to me?" Roy asked his friend Will. He and Will were playing cards when he said, "I don't like to scare Millie. But what if I get sick? Millie can't take care of me. How would I get up and around? Millie couldn't hold me up. I'm two times her size."

"Roy, maybe you won't always be so heavy. If you go on a diet like the doctor says, you'll lose weight," Will said.

"Yeah. And if I can't eat sweets, I'll get really thin," said Roy. "But I really like to eat sweets. I just like food, and I like to eat it. I'm 68 years old. I want to eat what I like, when I like. I don't care if I am fat."

"But you do care about Millie, don't you? And you care about Scott." Will looked over at the picture of Roy and Millie's five-year-old grandson.

"Of course I do. I love them."

"Then stay well for them, Roy. Stay well for them so you're around when that grandson of yours is playing football in high school."

"I hate getting old!" said Roy.

"Don't we all, old buddy. But we all must do it," said Will. "Now come on, let's play cards. It's your turn. Pick a card."

Back at Dr. Bell's

Roy visited the doctor again. The second test showed what Dr. Bell had thought it would.

"You do have diabetes, Roy, but the good news is that we caught it early. For now, diet, exercise, and losing weight are all you need to do. But it is very important to follow the diet I have given you."

"I'll try," said Roy.

The doctor looked hard and long at Roy. "No, Roy, you must do more than try. You must do it. This is very important. Diabetes is **serious**, but it can be cared for now with diet and exercise. However, if you are not serious about it, there can be some big problems later on. Your eyes, your heart, and your kidneys are just a few things that could be hurt later if you are not careful now."

Roy nodded his understanding.

"Working together, Roy, we will be able to do this." Dr. Bell smiled. "Now, let's go see the nurse about that diet and exercise program."

Roy Learns to Change

"I can't believe this!" Roy said to Millie that night. "My life is changing. I don't like change. Now I have to go on a diet. I can't eat your apple pie. I have to exercise."

"Roy!" said Millie, "don't be such a grump. I can make apple pie with sugar **substitute**. And as for exercise, we can take nice morning walks in the park together."

Roy smiled. "That's true."

His wife smiled back and pointed to the picture of their grandson. "The important things will still be the same."

serious *very important*

substitute *something used for another*

Words, Words, Words

A. Using the story, find an **antonym** for the words below. Remember, an antonym is a word that has the opposite meaning.

1. husband _____
2. fat _____
3. down _____
4. late _____
5. morning _____
6. young _____

B. Write the contraction for each pair of words below.

1. there is _____
2. I am _____
3. is not _____
4. I will _____
5. it is _____

Now write the pair of words for the contractions below.

6. we'll _____
7. you're _____
8. shouldn't _____
9. can't _____
10. wouldn't _____
11. weren't _____
12. couldn't _____
13. isn't _____
14. don't _____

Word Story:

You may have heard someone say, It's taboo! The person was saying that something should not be done. For example, in some countries it is taboo to talk about dead relatives. The word taboo *is a Polynesian word that means "a word or action not allowed."*

C. Some words have **short vowel sounds** like *sat, jet, pin, mop,* and *drum.* Some words have long vowel sounds like *make, beat, mile, coat,* and *tube.* Read the sentences below. Complete the sentences with long vowel sound words. Write your answers on the lines.

1. Sue wanted to (make, mend) the coat. _____

2. "Your wife was (smart, right)," said Dr. Bell. _____

3. Roy liked to eat (sugar, sweets). _____

Now complete the following sentences with short vowel sound words. Write your answers on the line.

4. What is his (name, address)? _____

5. Roy (woke, sat) up in bed. _____

6. He (had, needed) to go to the bathroom. _____

D. The letters **mb** can stand for the **m sound** as in the word *comb.* Put a √ next to the words in which the letters **mb sound** like **m.** The first one is done for you.

1. __√__ climb   2. _____ mumble   3. _____ lumber

4. _____ jumble   5. _____ numb   6. _____ crumb

Now write sentences for two of the **mb sound** words.

7. _____

_____

_____

_____

8. _____

_____

_____

_____

Understanding

A. Use the story and your own ideas to answer the questions below.

   1. Do you think Roy was mad when he learned he had diabetes? Why or why not?

      _____

      _____

   2. Do you think Roy was sad? Why or why not?

      _____

      _____

B. Read the sentences below. Put a √ next to the word or words that tell how Roy was feeling.

   1. Millie looked worried. Roy put his arm around his wife. "It'll be OK," he said. But he couldn't look into Millie's eyes. He didn't want her to see his tears.

     a. _____ sad   b. _____ happy   c. _____ proud

     d. _____ caring e. _____ afraid   f. _____ lonely

   2. "But I really like to eat sweets. I just like food, and I like to eat it. I'm 68 years old. I want to eat what I like, when I like. I don't care if I am fat."

     a. _____ happy b. _____ proud   c. _____ mad

Discussion

A. Read the story again. Then, answer the questions below.

1. What do you think is the main idea of the first part of the story called "Roy Sees a Problem"?

   _____

   _____

2. What do you think is the main idea of the last sentence in the story, "The important things will still be the same."

   _____

   _____

B. A **cause** is what makes something happen. The **effect** is what happens. Read the pairs of sentences below. One sentence shows the *cause.* Put **C** next to it. The other sentence shows the *effect.* Put **E** next to it. The first one is done for you.

1. __E__ Roy had to go to the bathroom.

   __C__ Roy woke up and got out of bed.

2. _____ Roy read some papers about diabetes.

   _____ Roy learned about diabetes.

3. _____ Roy was mad and sad for a while.

   _____ Roy found out he had to change his eating habits.

4. _____ Millie told Roy to see the doctor.

   _____ Roy was always tired and thirsty.

A Closer Look at the Food Pyramid

Did you know that there are **five** major food groups? The five food groups are:

1. **The bread, cereal, rice, and pasta group.** From this group, you could eat breads, waffles, pancakes, muffins, bagels, noodles, or rice.

2. **The vegetable group.** This group of food has very little fat. You could eat broccoli, carrots, collard greens, or spinach.

3. **The fruit group.** In this group, you could choose fruits such as apples, bananas, and oranges.

   Can you name some other fruits? Write the names below.

   _____

   _____

If you wrote *strawberries, watermelons,* or *plums,* you were right.

4. **The milk, yogurt, and cheese group.** This group has all the cheeses and other dairy products.

5. **The meat, poultry, fish, dry beans, eggs, and nuts group.** When you eat fish or eggs, you are eating from this food group. You can also choose beef, pork, or chicken.

This food guide is given to help you pick smart food choices each day. But choosing foods from each group may still not mean you are eating a healthy diet. You must also make sure you eat the right number of servings.

To help you with your choices, you sometimes see this food guide shown as a pyramid. It shows the Food Pyramid. Each food group is shown. It also shows the number of servings you should try to eat every day. If you follow this guide, you will be eating a healthy diet.

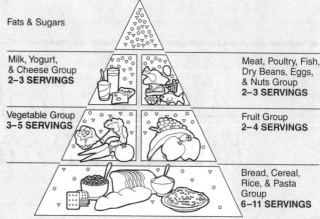

Use the pyramid to answer the questions below.

1. How many servings of fruit should you eat each day? _____

2. In what group would okra belong? _____

3. How many servings of meat or poultry can you have each day? _____

4. On Tuesday night, you made spaghetti with meat sauce for dinner. You also made a big salad with lettuce, tomato, and onions. What food groups did you have in your meal? _____

   _____

   What other foods could you have served to include all the food groups at this meal? _____

5. You pack a lunch for school or work. What could you pack to have one serving of all the food groups?

   Fruit group _____

   Bread group _____

   Vegetable group _____

   Milk group _____

   Meat group _____

LESSON 10

Office Work

Read this story to find out if you would like to be an office worker.

The Need for Office Workers

Good office workers will always be needed. Computers and other office machines will never replace them. However, these machines need office workers who can learn how to do many new things.

In the past, office workers did the same jobs all the time. They typed, filed, and answered phones. They often didn't have much contact with other people.

Today office jobs are changing. Office workers don't just handle paperwork. They handle **information.** They have to know much more. They also work with people more. Many of them help **managers** themselves. Some in time even become managers.

Today's office workers must know more and do more. They get better pay and **benefits** than in the past. They also have more chances to move to better jobs.

Office workers are needed in most businesses everywhere. So if you have to move, you will likely find office jobs in your new place.

information *facts and figures*

managers *people who are in charge of other people*

benefits *things that help*

If you are a good office worker, you can choose from many places to work. For example, you can work for a sales or service company, a bank, a school, or a hospital. You can work for a store, a factory, a law firm, or the government. You can work in a small or big office. Your job could be in a small town or a big city. You can also work full- or part-time.

Types of Office Workers

secretary *a type of office worker*

Juan is a general **secretary**. He does jobs that are needed in most offices. He **keyboards**. He keeps records. He takes notes. Juan talks with people in person, or on the telephone.

keyboards *types*

specialist *a person who has skills to do a certain job*

Marge is a **specialist**. She works in a law firm as a legal secretary. She works for a lawyer. Sometimes Marge finds information the lawyer needs. She helps prepare papers for people who are buying homes, doing wills, or signing contracts. She also helps prepare papers for people going to court.

medical assistant *a worker whose job is in a medical office, lab, or hospital*

Jake is a **medical assistant**. He works in a doctor's office. Jake sets up appointments and lab tests. He talks with doctors and patients. He checks medical charts and files them. He keeps records, sends out bills, and orders supplies.

Toni is also a medical assistant for a doctor. Toni's job is different from Jake's. She does some of the same office work that he does, but she spends more time helping the doctor with her patients. She talks to patients and writes down information for the doctor. She takes X rays and helps with lab tests. There are many jobs for medical assistants like Jake and Toni.

Needed Skills

No matter where you work as an office worker, you need certain skills. Keyboarding skills of at least 70 to 80 words per minute are needed. You will need to know how to use computers and fax machines. You will handle written information. You should write well, using good grammar and correct spelling. You must find and correct mistakes in written work. You will also use your math skills.

Office workers do many jobs each day. You need to be **organized**. You must choose what is most important to do and how to do it best. If you say you will do something, you must do it on time. If you see work that needs to be done, don't wait to be asked to do it.

organized *keeping things in order*

You will probably be working with people in your job. You need to be cheerful, friendly, and a good listener. You must speak well in person and on the phone. Try to dress neatly and be well-groomed.

Most office workers have to be team players because they may work in groups. Getting along with other people is important. It's also important to be loyal to a boss and to the company. For example, you must not tell people information that they are not supposed to know.

How to Become an Office Worker

For beginning office work, you will need a high school diploma or a GED. College work or other training is helpful. The training you need depends on the job you want.

Many schools or programs offer special training for certain jobs. Training can be anywhere from a few weeks to years. Classes in keyboarding, shorthand, computers, bookkeeping, accounting, office skills, and management can all be helpful.

Employers and business teachers can give you more information. And you may get training while on the job. Your boss or other workers may train you.

Words, Words, Words

A. Read the sentences below. Look for the word with the line under it. Write the word or words that it stands for. The first one is done for you.

Word Story:

The word résumé *is a French word. It means to make a summary. A* résumé *can be used when looking for a job. It is a summary of your work and skills.*

1. Computers help office workers. However, they will never replace <u>them</u>. _____**office workers**_____

2. Write down the date of your meeting. Make sure you keep <u>it</u>.

   _____

3. Most offices have fax machines. <u>They</u> can help secretaries save time. _____

4. Toni helped Mrs. Green with a lab test. Toni told <u>her</u> what to do. _____

5. Writing and spelling are important. <u>Those</u> are skills that office workers need. _____

B. The words *girl's car* tell that the car belongs to one girl. The words *girls' car* tell that the car belongs to more than one girl.

Add **'s** to show something belongs to one person.

Add **s'** to show something belongs to more than one person. Read the words below. Write the words with **'s** or **s'**.

1. the writing of the doctor _____

2. the offices of the workers _____

3. the skills of the players _____

4. the lab test of the girl _____

C. Some words have the letters **ar, er, ir, or,** and **ur.** These letters have the sounds you hear in *yard, fern, girl, storm,* and *burn.* Use **ar, er, or, ir,** or **ur** to complete each word.

1. Tomás was the f____st person to become a manag____.

2. C____rect any spelling mistakes that you find.

3. The school off____s many business classes.

4. She is a gen____al office work____.

5. Kelly works p____t-time for a school office.

6. The doct____ wrote in Mr. Varca's ch____t.

7. Tomás knew how to follow ____ders.

8. Her sister works in a law f____m.

9. The meeting will be held in M____ch.

D. The letters **ph** and **ng** can stand for the sounds you hear in *phone* and *along.* Use **ph** or **ng** to complete each word.

1. Office workers need good ____one skills.

2. The doctor's writi____ is not easy to read.

3. Gracie is usi____ the new computer.

4. Did you see the ____otos she took?

5. She made a gra____ for the doctor's report.

Understanding

A. A **fact** is something you know is true.

My sister can keyboard 80 words per minute.

An **opinion** is what you feel or believe.

My sister is a good office worker.

Write **F** if the sentence is a fact from the story.

Write **O** if the sentence is an opinion.

1. _____ Many schools offer classes in computers.

2. _____ Most bosses are hard to get along with.

3. _____ Office workers sometimes become managers.

4. _____ Women make better office workers than men do.

5. _____ Some office people work part-time.

6. _____ My sister would make a good manager.

B. Write your answers on the lines. Use the story and your own ideas to answer the questions.

1. What skills do you think an office worker needs to become a manager? _____

_____

2. Do you think computers will change office work in the future? In your own words, explain your answer. _____

_____

_____

Discussion

A. Read the questions below. Use the story to help you with your answers.

   1. What classes are helpful for office workers to take?

     _____

     _____

     _____

     _____

   2. What keyboarding skills should an office worker have?

     _____

     _____

     _____

     _____

B. Which of the following best tells about the **whole** story "Being an Office Worker"? Put a √ by your answer.

   1. _____ It's important for office workers to handle information using computers and office machines. There are many places for them to get training.

   2. _____ Today's office workers need to know more and do more. With good skills and training, they can work in many kinds of jobs. They can do general work or be specialists. They can become managers.

Steve Has an Interview

WORKPLACE · SKILLS ·

Read about Steve. He is interviewing for an office job.

Before the Interview

Steve answered the phone.

"Steve Brown?" a man asked. "I'm Mr. Mills from the East Clinic. We just received your **cover letter** and résumé for an office job. Your letter says you are free on Friday. Can you come to the clinic at 3:00 P.M. for an **interview**?"

"Yes, Mr. Mills. I'll be there."

When Steve hung up the phone, he was excited. Ever since his uncle had told him about the job openings at the new clinic, he wanted to apply for one. His uncle told him to send a cover letter first and ask for an interview. Steve called to find out the person who would be doing the interviews. He was told it was Mr. Mills and so he addressed his letter to him.

Getting Ready

That night Steve got ready for his interview. He chose a neat business suit and tie to wear. He also planned to take a notebook and another copy of his résumé with him.

cover letter *a letter sent when someone is seeking a job*

interview *a meeting about a job*

He had written the résumé weeks ago. The staff at his school's Jobs Center had helped him. The résumé showed his education. It told where he had worked, his outside activities, and three **references**. He had called the people beforehand to ask if he could use their names.

Steve was nervous because this was his first real interview. He knew that many people would be applying for a few jobs. Steve thought about his skills. He tried to think of questions Mr. Mills might ask. He wrote the questions down and practiced his answers. While he practiced, he watched himself in the mirror.

The Interview

Steve was at the clinic before 3:00. He didn't want to be late. Mr. Mills greeted him and took him into his office. He offered Steve a seat. Then he spent a few minutes reading Steve's résumé before he started asking questions.

"I see you're taking business classes at the community college. Most of your work has been office work in your uncle's medical supply business. You work there part-time. Why do you want a job at our clinic?"

Steve answered, "I've been working there for a few years. And I could probably be hired full-time. I like working in the medical field, and I enjoy office work. But I would like a job with many different things to do. I also want a job that lets me work more with people. I think your clinic could give me that."

"What kind of job did you have in mind?" Mr. Mills asked.

Steve wished he had taken the time to learn more about the clinic.

"Well, I heard that you had job openings. Because of my work, I think I could do many things in your clinic. I can keyboard 85 words a minute. I'm a good writer. I know how to handle written work. I head the school newspaper staff. I write memos for my uncle's company. I've also studied accounting and bookkeeping, so I could handle patient accounts and billing. I file and keep records well. I'm very organized, so I would be good at setting up appointments and meetings. And I already know a lot of medical words. That will help me."

"I see," Mr. Mills said. "Good writing and math skills are useful. Do you work with a computer, Steve? We use computers here."

"Yes, I've used computers at my uncle's company. But I think I need more work on that. I'm willing to learn."

Mr. Mills nodded. "Have you used a fax machine and **e-mail**? We also use them here."

e-mail *electronic mail sent on a computer*

Steve said, "Yes, I've used both."

Mr. Mills smiled. "Steve, what do you like to do when you are not working or are at school? Do you do any **volunteer** work?

volunteer *a person who offers help without pay*

Steve was surprised at those questions.

"Well, every year I help with the Special Olympics. And I've organized people in my church to visit older people in nursing homes and hospitals."

initiative *take the lead*

"That shows you take **initiative**," Mr. Mills said. "Are there any other things you would like to tell me about yourself?"

"Well, I really think I get along well with people. I like helping them. I hope that in any job here I would get a chance to work with people—patients, staff, or both."

"Good. How long do you plan to stay here, Steve, if you're hired?"

"If I do a good job and enjoy it, I plan to stay for quite a while."

"That's good, Steve. Do you have any questions you want to ask me?"

Steve asked a few questions about job duties and salary during the rest of the interview.

After the Interview

At the end of the interview, Steve thanked Mr. Mills. Mr. Mills told Steve he would be in touch with him.

relieved *less worried*

After it was all over, Steve felt **relieved**. He knew he had done the best he could. He had prepared for the interview. And he had answered all the questions clearly and honestly.

When he got home, Steve wrote Mr. Mills a thank-you note. He thanked him for the interview. He wrote that he would be interested in working at the clinic. Now there was nothing to do but wait!

Words, Words, Words

A. Read each sentence. Look for the word with the line under it. Put a √ next to the word or words that mean the same.

1. Your letter says you are <u>free</u> on Friday for an interview.

   a. ____ without cost

   b. ____ not busy

2. I could <u>handle</u> written work.

   a. ____ touch

   b. ____ work well with

3. I file and keep <u>records</u>.

   a. ____ disks to play music

   b. ____ information written down

4. I could handle <u>patient</u> accounts.

   a. ____ person seeing a doctor

   b. ____ able to wait

B. Read the sentences below. Some words sound the same but have different meanings. Write the word with the right meaning on the line.

1. I saw the manager a (weak, week) _____ ago.

2. Joe will (meet, meat) _____ you this afternoon.

3. (Would, Wood) _____ you like to ask me a question?

Word Story:

Alpha is the first letter in the Greek alphabet. The word alpha *is used for the first tests of software—the* alpha *version.*

4. We use many computers (here, hear) _____ .

5. Are (they're, there, their) _____ any job openings at the clinic?

C. Read each row of words below. Put a √ next to the two words in each row that have the same vowel sound.

1. a. _____ told   b. _____ got   c. _____ both

2. a. _____ few   b. _____ spent   c. _____ let

3. a. _____ plan   b. _____ staff   c. _____ all

4. a. _____ greet   b. _____ brief   c. _____ there

5. a. _____ take   b. _____ have   c. _____ wait

6. a. _____ think   b. _____ tie   c. _____ might

D. Read the sentences below. Choose a pair of letters to complete the words in the sentences. Use **ph, sh, th, ch,** or **ng**. These letters can stand for one sound. Make sure the words fit the meanings of the sentences.

1. He gets alo_____ with everyone in the office.

2. Please _____ow me how to use the fax machine.

3. He took a _____one message for his boss.

4. Steve wrote a _____ank-you letter.

5. I wi_____ I knew more about that job.

6. He kept in tou_____ with me by writing letters.

7. Mr. Mills hu_____ up his coat.

8. He had worked for his uncle for _____ree years.

Understanding

A. Answer the questions below. Use the story to help you.

1. What are the differences between Steve's job at the medical supply company and the job he wants at the clinic?

_____

_____

2. What is the same about the skills Steve uses in his job at his uncle's company and the skills he would use for the clinic job?

_____

_____

B. Give three reasons why Steve might be hired for a job at the clinic.

1. _____

2. _____

3. _____

C. Do you think Steve was ready for his interview with Mr. Mills? Explain your answer.

_____

_____

D. What might have happened if Steve had been late for his interview with Mr. Mills?

_____

_____

Discussion

A. Read the sentences below. Show the order in which things happened in the story. The first one is done for you.

_____ Steve received a call about an interview.

_____ Steve wrote a letter of thanks to Mr. Mills.

_____ Steve asked Mr. Mills questions about salary.

__1__ Steve arrived for the interview.

_____ Steve heard about jobs at the clinic.

_____ Mr. Mills asked Steve why he wanted a job.

_____ Steve sent a résumé and a cover letter .

B. Webbing helps you think up ideas. Fill in the empty circles with your ideas about interview questions.

A Closer Look at Job Interviews

W O R K P L A C E · SKILLS

You've read about Steve. To get ready for his job interview, he wrote down some questions he might be asked. He also wrote out some answers. By doing this, he felt ready for the interview. Read some of Steve's questions and answers.

1. What type of job do you want? _I like office work and working with people._

2. Do you want a full-time job? Do you want a part-time job?
   I want a full-time job.

3. What skills do you have to do this job? _I can keyboard 85 wpm, I write well, I get along with people, I follow directions._

4. What kind of training do you have for this job? _I take business classes at the community college._

5. What type of benefits do you want? _I would like to join a health plan and a savings or company retirement plan, and have vacation time._

Now, pretend you are going for a job interview. It may be a job that you're trying to get now or one you want in the future. Write down answers to the questions below. Doing this may help you in an interview. It may also help you make up a résumé to take to an interview.

1. What type of job do you want? _____

2. Does the job have a special name? _____

3. Why would you like to have this job? _____
_____

4. Do you need education for this job? _____

5. List schools you attended or training programs you took. List dates, diplomas, or degrees you have. _____
_____

6. What jobs have you had? (Write your employer's name, address, and phone number. Tell when you worked there. Tell what you did on the job.) _____
_____
_____

7. What skills do you have that will help you do the job? (Are you organized? Do you type well? Do you write and speak well? Do you have good phone skills?) _____
_____

8. What do you plan to do in the future that will help you do a job better? _____
_____

9. Give names, addresses, and phone numbers of three people (not relatives) who could tell an employer about you. (They are references for you.) _____
_____

Meet the Poets

Poetry is an old form of art. Some very early poems were really songs, but the music can no longer be found. The words in poems often make rhythms. Poetry has ideas of great meaning "packed" into a small piece of writing.

On the next few pages you will read six wonderful poems! The first three are by the African-American writers Maya Angelou and Langston Hughes. "Alone" is about the idea that no one can make it in this world alone. The poem "Woman Work" shows the busy life of a woman and her wish to find a restful place. "I, Too" is a poem about a man's hope to be accepted for who he is and not to be judged by the color of his skin.

Robert Frost's "Stopping by Woods on a Snowy Evening" is about a journey on a dark, lonely night.

The next group of poems are about people in the world of work. "Short-Order Cook" shows a man working hard and having fun doing it. And "Want Ads—Employment Opportunities" is about someone having trouble finding a good job.

Poets use words to paint pictures in your mind. As you read these poems, see what words the poets used to paint those pictures. Listen to hear the music of their words.

The Reading Corner

Maya Angelou was born in 1928. She is an African-American poet and novelist. She has also worked as a civil rights activist. At one time, she was even a nightclub performer. She was born in St. Louis but she spent most of her childhood with her grandmother in Arkansas. She later wrote a book about those years called *I Know Why the Caged Bird Sings*. In 1993 Maya Angelou read one of her poems at President Clinton's inauguration.

Alone

Lying, thinking
Last night
How to find my soul a home
Where water is not thirsty
And bread loaf is not stone
I came up with one thing
And I don't believe I'm wrong
That nobody,
But nobody
Can make it out here alone.

Alone, all alone
Nobody, but nobody
Can make it out here alone.
There are some millionaires
With money they can't use
Their wives run round like banshees
Their children sing the blues
They've got expensive doctors

But nobody
No, nobody
Can make it out here alone.

Alone, all alone
Nobody, but nobody
Can make it out here alone.

I'll tell you what I know
Storm clouds are gathering
This wind is gonna blow
The race of man is suffering
And I can hear the moan,
'Cause nobody,
But nobody
Can make it out here alone.

Alone, all alone
Nobody, but nobody
Can make it out here alone.

Woman Work

I've got the children to tend
The clothes to mend
The floor to mop
The food to shop
Then the chicken to fry
The baby to dry
I got company to feed
The garden to weed
I've got the shirts to press
The tots to dress
The cane to be cut
I gotta clean up this hut
Then see about the sick
And the cotton to pick.

Shine on me, sunshine
Rain on me, rain
Fall softly, dewdrops
And cool my brow again.

Storm, blow me from here
With your fiercest wind
Let me float across the sky
Till I can rest again.

Fall gently, snowflakes
Cover me with white
Cold icy kisses and
Let me rest tonight.

Sun, rain, curving sky
Mountain, oceans, leaf and stone
Star shine, moon glow
You're all that I can call my own.

Maya Angelou

Langston Hughes (1902–1967) wrote poetry, novels, children's books, screenplays, and newspaper columns. His poetry was strongly touched by the rhythms of jazz music. His first published poem was "The Negro Speaks of Rivers." It tells about the black people's experience. Read the poem below. It is another Langston Hughes poem about black people's experience in America.

I. Too

I, too, sing America.

I am the darker brother.
They send me to eat in the kitchen
When company comes,
But I laugh,
And eat well,
And grow strong.

Tomorrow,
I'll be at the table
When company comes.
Nobody'll dare
Say to me,
"Eat in the kitchen," Then.

Besides,
They'll see how beautiful I am
And be ashamed—

I, too, am America.

Langston Hughes

Robert Frost (1874–1963) was born in San Francisco but lived most of his life in New England. He attended college and in 1912 moved to England with his wife. His first two books of poems were published in England. They were very successful. He returned to the United States in 1915. He wrote many poems about the life and the land of New England.

Robert Frost was the first poet to read at a President's inauguration. He read at President Kennedy's inauguration in 1961. He won the Pulitzer Prize four times for his poetry. Read one of his poems below.

Stopping by Woods on a Snowy Evening

Whose woods these are I think I know.
His house is in the village though;
He will not see me stopping here
To watch his woods fill up with snow.

My little horse must think it queer
To stop without a farmhouse near
Between the woods and frozen lake
The darkest evening of the year.

He gives his harness bells a shake
To ask if there is some mistake.
The only other sound's the sweep
Of easy wind and downy flake.

The woods are lovely dark and deep,
But I have promises to keep,
And miles to go before I sleep,
And miles to go before I sleep.

Robert Frost

The Reading Corner

The following poems are about the workplace.

Read "Short-Order Cook" by Jim Daniels.

Short-Order Cook

An average joe comes in and orders
30 cheeseburgers and 30 fries.
I wait for him to pay before I start cooking,
He pays—
he ain't no average joe.

This grill is just big enough for 10 rows of 3.
I slap the burgers down,
throw two buckets of fries in the deep frier
and they pop pop spit spit . . .
psss . . .
The counter girls laugh.
I concentrate
It is the crucial point:
they are ready for the cheese.

My fingers shake as I tear off slices, toss
them on the burgers/fries done/dump/
refill buckets/burgers ready/flip
into buns, beat that melting cheese/wrap
burgers in plastic/into paper bags/fries done/
dump/fill 30 bags/bring them to the counter,
wipe sweat on sleeve, and smile at the counter girls.
I puff my chest out and bellow:
"30 cheeseburgers, 30 fries."
They look at me funny,
I grab a handful of ice, toss it in my mouth,
do a little dance, and walk back to the grill.
Pressure, responsibility, success.
30 cheeseburgers, 30 fries.

The poet Robert Garrison, born in 1945, wrote the next poem about looking for a job.

Want Ads—Employment Opportunities

Looking through the paper
There's sure a lot of jobs
I don't want.

Words, Words, Words

A. Read the lines below. Put a √ next to their meanings.

1. *But nobody*
    No, nobody
    Can make it out here alone.

    These lines mean

    a. _____ that the poet is afraid of being alone

    b. _____ that the poet is standing outside in the dark.

    c. _____ that people need someone else to help them get
    along in this world.

2. *An average joe comes in and orders*
    30 cheeseburgers and 30 fries.
    I wait for him to pay before I start cooking,
    He pays—
    he ain't no average joe.

    These lines mean

    a. _____ that the man is named Joe.

    b. _____ that the man can eat 30 cheeseburgers and 30 fries.

    c. _____ that the man is able to pay for what he orders and this
    makes him more than average.

3. *To cure their hearts of stone.*

This line means

a. ____ that some people have heartburn.

b. ____ that some people have hearts made of stone.

c. ____ that some people have no feelings for others and are not very kind.

B. One word can have many meanings. For example, the word *orange* can have different meanings.

She wore an *orange* dress.
The word *orange* means a color.

She ate an *orange* for lunch.
The word *orange* means a fruit to be eaten.

Read the sentences below. Write in your own words the different meanings for the underlined words.

1. I am the <u>darker</u> brother _____

_____

_____

_____

_____

2. The woods are lovely <u>dark</u> and deep _____

_____

_____

_____

_____

Understanding

A. Put a √ next to your answers. Use the poems to help you.

1. Where does the woman live in the poem "Woman Work"?

   a. _____ the city   b. _____ on a farm

2. How does the horse feel in the poem "Stopping by Woods on a Snowy Evening"?

   a. _____ The horse likes being in the snow.

   b. _____ The horse thinks it's very odd to stop.

3. Who or what is ready for the cheese in the poem "Short-Order Cook"?

   a. _____ the hamburgers   b. _____ the counter girls

B. Use the poems to help you answer the questions below.

1. Why do you think the speaker in the poem "Stopping by Woods on a Snowy Evening" stopped in the woods?

   _____

   _____

2. Is the speaker in the poem "Want Ads—Employment Opportunities" having much luck finding a job?

   _____

   _____

3. How does the short-order cook feel about his job?

   _____

   _____

You Can Write a Poem

On the lines below, try your hand at writing a poem. You can write about anything. It can be a poem about your job. It can be a poem about your family. It can be a poem about how you feel. You can look to nature and write about the seasons or a garden or the sky. Listen to your favorite song. It, too, is a form of poetry. Remember, a poem doesn't have to rhyme. It tells how you feel or think about something. And don't forget a title.

_____

_____

_____

_____

_____

_____

_____

_____

A. Put a √ next to the words with the same **g sound**
as the first word.

   1. **grabbed** a. _____ magic   b. _____ strange   c. _____ grace

   2. **large**   a. _____ frogs   b. _____ page   c. _____ gone

B. Put a √ next to the words with the same **c sound**
as the first word.

   3. **car**   a. _____ catalog b. _____ race   c. _____ certain

   4. **face**   a. _____ clump b. _____ carton   c. _____ dance

C. Put a √ next to the synonym for the first word.

   5. **heavy**   a. _____ thin   b. _____ overweight

   6. **sad**   a. _____ unhappy   b. _____ glad

D. Put a √ next to the antonym for the first word.

   7. **big**   a. _____ large   b. _____ small

   8. **near**   a. _____ close   b. _____ far

E. Put a √ next to the two words that sound the same but have
different meanings in each line.

   9. a. _____ now   b. _____ knows   c. _____ nose   d. _____ know

   10. a. _____ sum   b. _____ sun   c. _____ some   d. _____ send

   11. a. _____ two   b. _____ too   c. _____ tool   d. _____ toes

   12. a. _____ at   b. _____ ate   c. _____ eight   d. _____ night

F. Add a prefix to the following words to give them
the opposite meanings.

   13. wanted _____

   14. known _____

G. Put a √ next to your answer.

15. The thunder scared the dog. It _____ under the bed.

_____ played   _____ ran   _____ slept

16. Helen had a _____ garden. She picked them to put in a vase. They had a beautiful scent.

_____ cabbage   _____ rose   _____ vegetables

H. Read the story. Put a √ next to the best answer.

Hal was driving his car. He heard a loud sound. His car suddenly swayed. Then the car bumped. It was his front tire going flat. He carefully lifted his foot from the pedal. He slowed down. Then, he eased the car off the road and came to a stop. Just his luck. He was late for an appointment and now he had to change a flat tire.

17. What was the story mostly about?

_____ car safety

_____ a tire going flat

_____ Hal's appointment

18. What would be a good title for this story?

_____ Hal's Unlucky Day

_____ How to Fix a Flat Tire

_____ Driving Without a Spare

I. Put a √ next to the meaning for the underlined word in the sentence.

19. Some people say he has a heart of stone.

a. _____ a large pebble   b. _____ unfeeling

20. Alan owns a computer company.

a. _____ a business   b. _____ people who come to visit

GLOSSARY

afford   to have enough money to buy something

aide   a helper

amounts   how much or how many

apprentice   someone who learns a job from another person

attended   was there

badges   name pins that are worn to be seen by others

benefits   things that help

bracelet   a band worn on the arm or wrist

budget   a plan for how much money you need and can spend

catalog store   a store that lists in a book the things it has to sell

cereal   a food from grain

chart   a paper which lists numbers, letters, or colors and gives information

content   being happy or feeling OK

cover letter   a letter sent when someone is seeking a job

decorations   writing, flowers, or designs on a cake

dessert   food served at the end of a meal

destination   a place someone is trying to reach

diet   a special food plan

diploma   a paper showing completed studies

disease   a problem in your body that makes you sick and causes your body not to work right

divide   to cut into parts

eager   to really want to do something

e-mail   electronic mail sent on a computer

equivalency   equal in value

events   happenings

glucose   sometimes called *blood sugar*; the sugar you eat turns into this once it is in your blood; it gives you energy

habits   the way people do things

heroes   very brave people

hobby   a favorite thing to do

homeland   your own country; the country where you were born

ID   a paper or badge showing who a person is

imagination   an active mind

information   facts and figures

initiative   take the lead

insulin   something found in your body that is needed to help change blood sugar into energy

interview   a meeting about a job

keyboards   types

managers	people who are in charge of other people	**route**	way or road
measure	to find the right amount	**scared**	afraid
medical assistant	a worker whose job is in a medical office, lab, or hospital	**secretary**	a type of office worker
		security deposit	money given to hold something
neighbor	someone who lives nearby	**serious**	very important
normal	the way things should be	**skills**	ways to do things
notes	written-down information	**specialist**	a person who has skills to do a certain job
operator	a person who answers the phone for a company	**staff**	a group of workers
organized	keeping things in order	**starch**	something found in foods like potatoes or noodles and used by the body the same way it uses sugar
parent-teacher conference	a school meeting between a child's teacher and his or her parents		
		stiff	hard to bend
patient	willing to wait	**stomach**	the body's food sac
plastic	material that can be easily shaped	**strict**	follow rules carefully
		student	a person in school
practice	do again and again	**sublet**	to rent to another for a short amount of time in the lease
prevent	stop from happening		
proud	happy or pleased with	**substitute**	something used for another
		succeeded	turned out OK
questions	things that people ask		
range	a group of numbers that have a beginning and end	**thirsty**	needing a drink of water
		trouble-shooting	directions on how to solve problems with an item such as an iron, a TV, or a CD player
receipt	a paper that shows you bought something and how much you paid for it		
		urine	body water that comes out when you go to the bathroom
recipes	cooking directions		
references	the names of people who can tell an employer about your work	**volunteer**	a person who offers help without pay
registration card	a card that comes with a product such an iron, a TV, or a CD player. When mailed into the company, the item is recorded for any later repairs.	**warranty**	a written promise a company gives to a buyer for certain repairs to a product such as a TV or an iron
		wisely	knowing about
relieved	less worried	**wrong**	not right

Your answers may be different for the Understanding and Discussion parts. Sample answers are given.

Lesson 1
Words, Words, Words
A. 2. does not 3. did not 4. I am 5. they are
B. 2. Marta's friend 3. Pedro's book
    4. David's classroom 5. Helena's child
    6. Steve's car 7. school's letter
C. 2. better 3. class 4. husband 5. help
D. 2. writing 3. back 4. wrong 5. check
    6. scissors
E. 1–3 Sample answers: 1. He went to the
    conference. 2. He had the wrong answer.
    3. I have her address.

Understanding
A. 2. O 3. F 4. F 5. O 6. F 7. F 8. F
B. 1. d 2. c

Discussion
A. ask questions; help with homework; talk
    to the teacher; have child go to school
    every day
B. 1. they will help him with his homework;
    go to parent-teacher conferences; ask
    him questions about school; ask to see
    his work.
    2. she felt better; she knew what questions
    to ask Ms. Chang; she knew what
    questions Ms. Chang might ask her; she
    knew to ask David questions before she
    went; she was able to get Pedro to go
    with her.

Lesson 2
Words, Words, Words
A. 3. S 4. A 5. A 6. A 7. A 8. A 9. S 10. S
B. 2. bed time 3. an other 4. story time
    5. bill boards 6. for ever
C. 2. donut 3. We 4. meet 5. wake
    6. paper 7. cake 8. jeep
D. 2. ch 3. th 4. ch, ch 5. th 6. ch 7. th
    8. th 9. Ch, ch

Understanding
A. 1. Children who are read to will know more
    words and be better readers than
    children who are not read to.
    2. The types of books that are read are
    different and the amount of time you
    spend.
B. 1. a 2. b

Discussion
A. 1. You can start reading to a baby. Any age
    is a good time to start reading aloud to a
    child.
    2. Good books for children are picture
    books; books that a child picks out;
    stories about subjects the child likes.
B. 1. O 2. O 3. F 4. O 5. O 6. O

Special Feature: A Closer Look at the Dictionary
A. 1. Yes 2. Yes 3. No 4. No 5. Yes 6. No
B. 1. mat 2. match 3. matter 4. meal
    5. meant 6. meat 7. meets 8. metal
C. 1. Guide words tell you what words will be
    on that page in the dictionary.
    2. You can learn their meaning; the way to
    say them; the part of speech.

Lesson 3
Words, Words, Words
A. 1. couldn't 2. you're 3. isn't 4. aren't
    5. they're
B. 1. ck 2. wr 3. ck 4. wr 5. ck 6. sc
C. 1. cake 2. beat 3. ice 4. go 5. tube
    6. rake 7. write 8. three
D. 2. four, for 3. new, knew 4. knows, nose
    5. two, too 6. flour, flower 7. sun, son,
    8. eight, ate 9. sum, some 10. blew, blue

Understanding
A. 1. F 2. O 3. F 4. F 5. F 6. O 7. F 8. O
B. 1. a 2. a 3. b

Discussion

A. 1. She was a little girl.
2. Arlene's mother taught her to buy wisely.
3. She read about them in the newspaper.

B. read books; read newspapers; went to classes; learned from her mother.

Lesson 4

Words, Words, Words

A. 1. A 2. S 3. A 4. A 5. A 6. A 7. A 8. S
9. A 10. A

B. 1. route 2. weigh 3. knew 4. for 5. read
6. sore 7. made

C. 1, 6, 11 Long o 4, 5, 8, 10, 12

D. 3. gate 4. page 5. gun 6. germs 7. goat

Understanding

A. 1. She wanted to be well known. She wanted to be like her grandmother. She wanted to be famous.
2. Luka and Mr. Schmidt were now partners.
3. She was happy.

B. 1. She will continue to make cakes and become well known. She will own many bakeries.
2. He will retire or he will open more bakeries with Luka.

Discussion

A. 1. Mr. Gomez, the bus driver 2. early evening
3. her Gran Petroni 4. he died 5. A 6. Mr. Schmidt 7. business and baking 8. someone who studies and learns a skill from another who is very good at that skill

B. Gran Petroni came from another country with cooking skills and recipes. She shared her knowledge with her granddaughter because she could no longer do the baking with her stiff hands. This sort of knowledge is usually passed down to the next generation.

Special Feature You Can Tell What's Happening

A. 1. in a front yard 2. fall or early winter 3. 2
4. They are sitting outside their house and talking. 5. happy

B. Answers will vary.

Lesson 5

Words, Words, Words

A. 1. reread He will reread the story.
2. unclean The desk top is unclean.

3. unknown The reason for the accident is unknown.

B. 2. b 3. b 4. b 5. a

C. 3. ea 4. ee 5. ea 6. ea 7. ea

D. 1. gn 2. ck 3. sc 4. kn 5. wr 6. ck 7. kn

Understanding

A. 1. O 2. F 3. F 4. O 5. F 6. O 7. F 8. F 9. F

B. Yes. They can afford it.

Discussion

A. 1. b 2. c

B. 1. They wanted a place of their own.
2. They had only one car.
3. They wanted to know what they might be getting into. They wanted to know their responsibilities and the landlord's.
4. They could afford the rent and the security deposit.

Special Feature A Closer Look at a Lease

A. 1. first day of the month 2. give one month's notice 3. electricity/gas 4. Anita and Rob
5. get landlord's OK 6. ask the landlord 7. the landlord 8. $200

Lesson 6

Words, Words, Words

A. 1. b 2. a 3. b 4. b 5. a

B. 1. c 2. a 3. b 4. c

C. 2. S 3. L 4. L 5. S

D. 1. k 2. s 3. k 4. k 5. s

E. 1. j 2. g 3. g 4. j 5. g 6. g 7. j 8. g
9. g 10. j

Understanding

A. 1. It cost less than new furniture. They didn't have much money to spend. 2. smoke detectors; safety locks 3. file cabinet or box; safe deposit box 4. shop at garage sales; use coupons

B. 1. 2-year warranty; they shut off 2. price; features

Discussion

A. 1. N 2. Y 3. Y

B. 1. keep the receipt and the warranty where they could find it if they needed it
2. take the receipt to the Service Center
3. bring back the work order to pick up the iron

Special Feature You Can Follow Directions

1. 23 2. Stop #3 at Clark St. and Robin Ave.
3. South 4. Before 8:05 A.M. 5. Stop #3 at Clark

St. and Robin Ave.　6. By 6:35 A.M.　7. Stop #1 at Clark St. and Poplar Rd.　Anita will need to walk to St. Luke's.　8. By 5:15 P.M.　9. Stop #4 at Clark St. and Red Rd.　10. From 3 P.M. to 4:25 P.M. or 1 hr. and 25 min.

Lesson 7
Words, Words, Words
A.　1. b　2. b
B.　1, 2, 4, 5, 9, 10, 14　17. paper work　18. basket ball　19. hand book　20. book store
C.　1. waited　2. stayed　3. day　4. rain　5. gray
D.　1. wr　2. sc　3. kn　4. wr　5. sc　6. kn　7. gn　8. gn　9. kn　10. wr

Understanding
A.　1. b　2. a　3. c
B.　1. They were worn on the wrist.　They were made of plastic.
　　2. They had to wear an ID badge.

Discussion
A.　1. a. ID bracelets　b. teach parents the hospital rules　c. name badges　d. never leave them alone　2. Ohio　3. look for the ID badge　4. to the nursery　5. to keep them safe
B.　They can footprint them and match the footprint to a badge.　They can take a picture of the parents and the baby and keep it on the records.　They can have everyone wear an ID bracelet or badge.

You Can Solve the Problem
Step 1:　The medicine will help Sue.　Once-in-a-lifetime problem
Step 2:　a. It will make her sick.　It will be hard to care for her children.　She will really need help. She cannot pay for day care.　Her husband works in the day.　Her family does not live near.
b. If her husband can find a way to help.　If her family can find a way to help.　If she does not take the medicine she will get cancer again for sure.
Step 3:　The other choices are:　Not to take the medicine.　Look at the family's money.　Maybe they can get a baby-sitter to help.　Ask if a family member can visit and help.　See if the husband can work less or work different hours.　See if the husband can stay home on Sue's worst days.
Step 4:　Best to Worst:　3, 4, 2 ,5, 1.
Step 5:　3 or 4.

Step 6:　Sue's family may be able to help.　Her husband may be able to help.　They may lose some money, but Sue will be taken care of.　She will have a better chance to stay well.

Lesson 8
Words, Words, Words
A.　1. a　2. b　3. b　4. b　5. a
B.　1. a, b, d　2. a, c　3. a, c, d　4. a, c
C.　1. e　2. i　3. e　4. e　5. i　6. e　7. e　8. i
D.　1. kn　2. ck　3. ck　4. wr

Understanding
A.　1. a　2. b　3. a
B.　1. F　2. O　3. O　4. F

Discussion
A.　1.With Type I you have to take shots.　With Type II you can control it with diet and exercise. Type I appears in children.　Type II usually occurs in adults.
　　2. People over 65 can get diabetes and should watch for the signs.
　　3. People overweight, in a certain age group, have family members with diabetes, women who had babies over 10 lbs.
B.　1

Lesson 9
Words, Words, Words
A.　1. wife　2. thin　3. up　4. early　5. evening　6. old
B.　1. there's　2. I'm　3. isn't　4. I'll　5. it's　6. we will　7. you are　8. should not　9. cannot　10. would not　11. were not　12. could not　13. is not　14. do not
C.　1. make　2. right　3. sweets　4. address　5. sat　6. had
D.　5, 6.　7 and 8: Sentences will vary.

Understanding
A.　1. Yes, he didn't want to change the way he lived or what he ate.　2. Yes, he was afraid for himself and his wife.　He cried when he knew he might have diabetes.　He was scared.
B.　1. a, d, e　2. c

Discussion

A. 1. The main idea is that Roy begins to realize he might have a health problem.   2. Even though Roy has to change the way he eats and has to diet and exercise, he still has his family and their love.

B. 2. C, E   3. E, C   4. E, C

Special Feature A Closer Look at the Food Pyramid

3. kiwi fruit, pears, peaches, watermelons, grapefruits, grapes

1. 2–4 servings   2. vegetables   3. 2–3 servings meat or poultry   4. bread, meat, vegetable; You could have served some cheese and grapes for dessert. This would have taken care of your milk and fruit groups.   5. Fruit: apples; Bread: a bagel; Vegetable: slices of tomato; Milk: a slice of cheese; Meat: 2 slices of turkey.

Lesson 10

Words, Words, Words

A. 2. date   3. fax machines   4. Mrs. Green
5. writing and spelling

B. 1. doctor's writing   2. workers' offices
3. players' skills   4. girl's lab test

C. 1. ir, er   2. or   3. er   4. er, er   5. ar
6. or, ar   7. or   8. ir   9. ar

D. 1. ph   2. ng   3. ng   4. ph   5. ph

Understanding

A. 1. F   2. O   3. F   4. O   5. F   6. O

B. 1. people skills—able to get along with people, good writing and speaking skills, good organizational skills   2. Yes, they will help with faster communication.   No, they will not go any further than how they are used now.

Discussion

A. 1. keyboarding, math, grammar, business communication   2. be able to keyboard at least 70 to 80 words per minute

B. 2

Lesson 11

Words, Words, Words

A. 1. b   2. b   3. b   4. a

B. 1. week   2. meet   3. Would   4. here   5. there

C. 1. a, c   2. b, c   3. a, b   4. a, b   5. a, c   6. b, c

D. 1. ng   2. sh   3. ph   4. th   5. sh   6. ch   7. ng
8. th

Understanding

A. 1. He will work with people. He will do accounts. It will be full-time.   2. He will need keyboarding, writing, math, and organizational skills.

B. 1. He has good keyboarding skills.   2. He writes well.   3. He has office job experience.

C. Yes, he had questions and answers prepared. He dressed correctly for an interview.   No, he did not know as much as he should have about the clinic.

D. He would have made a bad impression on Mr. Mills.   Mr. Mills may have left for the day.   Mr. Mills may have had another appointment and could not interview Steve.

Discussion

A. a. 3   b. 7   c. 6   d. 4   e. 1   f. 5   g. 2

B. Why do you want this job?   What other jobs have you had in this field?   Can you keyboard?   What types of classes have you taken?   Can you work full-time?   Can you work overtime?

Special Feature: A Closer Look At Job Interviews

1–10 Answers will vary.

The Reading Corner

Words, Words, Words

A. 1. c   2. c   3. c

B. 1. The darker brother is the black brother.
2. Dark means no light, or nighttime.

Understanding

1. b   2. b   3. a

Discussion

1. The speaker wanted to look at the pretty woods.   The speaker wanted to rest.   The speaker wanted to think about life.   The speaker needed to be alone.   2. No.

3. He likes his job.   He enjoys what he is doing. He has fun on the job.